Simple
Vegetable
Growing

Other Concorde Books

Photo courtesy Thompson & Morgan (Ipswich) Limited

Simple Vegetable Growing

Roy Genders

WARD LOCK LIMITED · LONDON

Contents

Introduction

Every day fresh vegetables seem to cost more, and every year frozen vegetables seem to become more tasteless. Scarcely surprising then, that we are now in the middle of the biggest boom in 'growing your own' ever known.

It's not just a myth that shop-bought vegetables taste dull. The criterion by which their growers judge them is whether they will look good and keep well. Flavour is often incompatible with these qualities.

When you grow your own you can go for flavour and you can grow dozens of unusual varieties of vegetables that you seldom meet in the shops.

There's no secret to success with vegetables. You just need to know what to do and when to do it. This book explains in simple and practical terms all you need to know to grow the finest vegetables you've ever tasted.

With good management you can keep the family in garden-fresh vegetables the whole year round. If you have a deep-freeze you can store summer crops to eat out of season ▶

PART I THE VEGETABLE GARDEN

1 Designing and Planning the Garden

The first requirement for growing vegetables is to provide an open, sunny situation for they will not grow well where the ground is partially shaded by mature trees and buildings. It is also important that, where early spring crops are required, the plants receive their share of the early sunshine, not only for their growth but to warm the soil before planting. The next requirement is some shelter from cold prevailing winds, especially if early crops are to be grown and the plants are to be set out with the expectation that they can enjoy a long period of growth to bring them to maturity at the time required. To protect the plants against cold winds, it is advisable to erect 5 ft. high inter-woven fencing or wattle hurdles on the sides from which the prevailing winds blow and these should be held in place with strong stakes. This form of fencing is preferable to planting a hedge which will not only require constant attention but will also use up moisture and nourishment required by the vegetables.

If the vegetable garden is divided from the rest of the garden by a screen of rustic poles, rambler roses may be grown against it, or wooden laths may be fastened to the screen at intervals of 15 in. and runner beans grown up them to a height of 6–8 ft. They will provide beauty with their flowers and foliage and the household with delicious beans to use during late summer and autumn.

If there is room for a small greenhouse and frames, then

select a place to erect them where they will receive the maximum amount of sunlight. To grow tomatoes and to bring on early seedlings both a greenhouse and a cold frame will be indispensable, for it will then be possible to raise one's own plants and to harden them before planting out. The plants will then get away to a good start without check and reach maturity in the quickest time.

Let the greenhouse and frame be erected at one side of the vegetable garden where they will receive ample sunlight and, in one corner, make a compost pit where lawn mowings, leaves, clearings from ditches, decayed vegetable refuse and possibly some poultry or horse manure can be collected to form compost which will be ready to dig into the soil when required. Here, all these humus-forming materials can be stored and, as the heap is built up, some peat and used hops may also be added so that when the soil is being prepared in autumn and spring, there will be available plenty of well composted humus to fork into the soil without which vegetables will not grow well. Vegetables should not even be attempted without there being available a good supply of humus-forming materials.

There should also be room to make a small seed bed where those vegetables to be planted for later maturity may be raised from seed sown in spring. Here, too, may be raised early plants by covering them with cloches which may be used later to raise early beans and peas and those other vegetables which require protection from late frosts and cold winds (e.g. marrows).

Rotation of Crops

The ground to be used for vegetables should be divided into four sections for a four-course rotation of cropping to ensure healthier and heavier crops. The vegetables will enjoy a change of ground every year which will not only prevent pests and diseases particular to a certain plant from building up but will also enable each vegetable to make full use of the various plant foods so necessary for its health and vitality.

Good paths are essential in any vegetable garden. These may be made of cut paving stone, bricks or gravel chippings, and will enable onions and radishes to be pulled or a cabbage

A well-managed vegetable garden. Note the hedge which helps protect the crops from cold winds in early spring. A fence would do as well. Three different varieties of cabbage are shown here

or lettuce cut without the need to change one's shoes during wet weather and without the need to tread on and consolidate the soil to the detriment of the crops. Good paths will also enable a barrow and possibly a push hoe or cultivator to be moved about the garden with the maximum of ease. Path making can be done in stages, when and as garden work permits, and the only tools needed will be a spade and a builder's spirit level to ensure that the path will be laid as straight and as level as possible.

The vegetable garden should be made up of four plots – one for potatoes; another for winter greens; one for peas and beans with salad crops between the rows; and one for root-crops such as turnips, parsnips and carrots to use during winter. They should follow rotational cropping as follows:

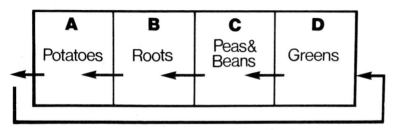

Diagrammatic representation of crop rotation. Crop rotation is most important: if it is not practised serious diseases will build up in the soil and the vegetable garden become useless

If the soil is well manured for potatoes, planting early, second early and main crop varieties, the potatoes will by their cultivations clean the ground and, by moving them round, this will ensure that the vegetable garden remains free from perennial weeds and that the soil remains in a friable condition. A heavy application of manure or compost for potatoes each year will mean that only limited supplies will be needed for other crops during the next 3 years and until the ground is made ready for potatoes again.

Root crops should follow potatoes for they grow best in a soil that has been manured for a previous crop. Fresh manure causes the roots to grow forked whilst it is also detrimental to their keeping qualities.

Follow root-crops with the legumes (beans and peas) for

they will leave the soil richer in nitrogen and this will be available to the greens to follow. This is due to the ability of their root nodules to fix the nitrogen in the soil. The greens in turn should be followed by potatoes.

By following the four-course rotation, each crop will make full use of the available plant foods but, to maintain the soil in good 'heart', it is important to see that it does not lack lime. If lime is not present, the inert plant foods stored up in the soil with the application of various manures and fertilizers will not be released to the growing crops and, however well the ground has been manured, the plants will obtain little benefit. Potatoes, however, prefer an acid soil so it is advisable to lime each plot separately after it has grown a potato crop. The correct use of lime will mean that there will be no wastage of fertilizers and less heavy applications will be required than if lime is not present.

Not only does rotational cropping maintain a balance between the various plant foods but the different methods of cultivation required by each group of plants will ensure that the soil is thoroughly tilled and to a considerable depth rather than merely on the surface. This will open up and aerate the soil and enable bacteria to obtain the supplies of oxygen so necessary to convert the manures and fertilizers into food which can be readily absorbed by the crops. Rotation will also prevent the accumulation of those pests and diseases of the soil which may be endemic to one group of plants and are known as 'soil sickness'.

Intensive Cropping

Where the area of ground to be given to vegetables is small, it must be cropped intensively and this means inter-cropping, i.e. planting crops between other crops so that one crop is developing whilst another is reaching maturity. However, situation and climate will play a part in this and in Somerset and Devon it is possible to obtain three crops a year from the same piece of ground compared with only one in parts of Yorkshire and Durham unless cloches are used. In the South-West where frosts rarely cause damage to winter lettuce and broccoli, these crops are grown to harvest in early spring, to be followed by French beans which are sown early in April as the ground is cleared, and by quickly maturing cauliflowers or cabbages, then by broccoli to cut in spring. Here, these crops follow potatoes so that rotation of cropping takes place in only 2 years. But the programme is followed just the same.

In less favoured areas, inter-cropping assumes a greater importance and here it will also be advisable to bring on the plants under glass, making use of cloches to start them off whilst spring frosts are still troublesome. In this way, at least a month's start will be gained over plants raised outdoors. In northern districts, quick-maturing varieties are now making it possible to obtain additional crops in a season. At the same time, sowings should be made in frames and under cloches so that as soon as one crop has been harvested, further plantings will be ready to take its place. Every day saved in bringing the crop to maturity will make for greater productivity and this is especially important if the garden is small. Spring cabbage may be followed by French beans with carrots sown alongside and followed by hardy winter broccoli which will give all the year round cropping.

Again, early potatoes or peas can be followed by lettuce, autumn cauliflowers or winter cabbage. It is not necessary to allow the ground to remain idle after harvesting the early crops. Well-cultivated land may be kept continuously productive, following rotational cropping as widely as possible though quick-maturing 'catch' crops may be grown in all parts of the garden wherever the opportunity presents itself. This is made possible by the introduction of new vegetables of quick maturity and of compact habit which are ideal for the small garden.

Keeping Records

When sowing under glass or in the open ground, make a note of the date of sowing and place a small wooden label in the ground at the end of each row. By keeping a record of sowing times and of varieties, it will be possible to find out the time taken for germination and it will be additionally helpful if day-to-day records of the weather are also kept. The correct sowing time for each crop may then be determined. In this way the plants will not occupy the boxes or frames longer than necessary, nor the open ground rows thereby causing them to become 'drawn' and starved of plant food before they can be moved to the open ground where they are to grow to maturity. This will usually be dictated by weather conditions. Again, delayed sowing may mean the loss of valuable time in harvesting the crop with the result that there may not be time for the growing of other crops that season.

Cropping table

	VARIETY	WHEN TO SOW	TO MATURE
Beet	Avon Early	April–May	Sept.–Nov.
Broad Bean	The Midget	October	May–June
Broccoli	Leamington	August	March–April
(Large heading)	Royal Oak	June	May–June
Broccoli (Sprouting)	Dwarf Green Curled	April	Nov.–March
Brussels sprouts	Avon Cross	March	Nov.–Feb.
	Peer Gynt	Early March	Sept.–Nov.
Cabbage	Primo	April	Aug.–Oct.
	Tozanda	March	Aug.–Sept.
	Sentinel	July	March–May
Cauliflower	Dwarf Monarch	April	Oct.–Nov.
	*Early Snowball	February	June–July
	All Year Round	April	Aug.–Sept.
French bean	Earligreen	Mid-April	July
Kale	Dwarf Curled	April	Nov.–March
Lettuce	Buttercrunch	April	June–July
	Tom Thumb	March	June–July
Pea	Onward	April	August
	Meteor	October	June
	Histon Mini	April	July
Runner bean	Hammond's Dwarf	Late April	Aug.–Sept.
Savoy	Asmer Shortie	March	Oct.–Dec.
Turnip	Golden Ball	March	Oct.–Nov.
Vegetable Marrow	Gold Nugget	April	July–Sept.

All these vegetables are of compact habit and quick to mature for they do not take as long a time as the more robust varieties to complete their growth.

* *Sow under glass.*

Do not attempt to grow too many varieties and do not raise more plants than you expect to use, though allowance should be made for losses due to adverse weather and other factors. Have a number of plants in readiness to fill in any gaps so as to make the maximum use of the ground. It will be advisable to grow a few different varieties each year so that one may discover which will crop best in the particular soil of one's garden, for the old adage 'horses for courses' very much applies to vegetable growing.

To make vegetable growing really worthwhile you need a succession of crops through the year. This picture shows three rows of carrots each sown a fortnight apart, beetroot in the centre nearing maturity and seedling lettuces planted to replace a crop that has already been gathered

2 Preparation of the Soil

It is rarely possible to find a garden where the soil is in exactly the right condition to grow good crops of vegetables. Usually it will be too heavy and badly drained so that excess moisture remains about the roots of the plants in winter, causing them to decay and autumn-sown peas and broad beans will be unable to survive such conditions. Or the soil may be dry and sandy and lacking in moisture so that the crops make little headway during the drier summer months when growth should be most vigorous. Some soils lack lime whilst others contain an excess, a condition that must be corrected to ensure heavy crops.

Soil Testing

The soil of every garden differs from the next but as a general rule soils may be divided into four main groups: (1) those of a clay nature, containing about $33\frac{1}{3}$ per cent clay particles; (2) those which may be classed as rich loam, containing no more than about 20 per cent clay; (3) those classed as light and containing about 75 per cent sand; and (4) calcareous soils which have a high chalk or lime content and which are generally 'hot' shallow soils. All soils differ however slightly, in that some are too acid (lacking in lime) whilst others are too alkaline (containing too much lime) so that the first necessity is to discover the pH value. pH stands for the hydrogen ion concentration of moisture in the soil and the acidity or alkalinity varies accordingly.

16

Intercropping. Here lettuces are being grown on the ridges thrown up from the celery trenches. Once the lettuces are cropped the earth is returned to the trenches to blanch the celery

Simple soil testing may be done at home using an indicator kit which consists of a bottle of indicator solution; a quantity of barium sulphate; glass test tubes; some distilled water; and a colour chart all housed in a compact wooden box in which the tubes stand upright.

The soil to be tested should be in a friable condition and be placed in the tube (half-full) with a spatula. To the soil add a small amount of barium sulphate, then fill almost to the top with distilled water and add a few drops of indicator. Place a rubber stopper into the end of the tube, shake up the contents and allow to settle, then compare the colour to that of the chart. Where the soil shows a lime deficiency, give 7 lb. of lime (hydrated) per 100 sq. ft. of ground area for each hydrogen ion value. Brassica crops require a soil of a high lime content, so do peas and beans, and for most crops the land should be well limed in winter.

Apart from its ability to correct the acidity of soil, lime has the power of being able to release the various plant foods pent up in the soil so that well manured land will not be beneficial to the growing crops unless lime is present to unlock the food content. Again, lime is able to improve the physical condition of the soil by breaking up the clay particles. For a heavy soil an application of caustic lime (unhydrated) will by its vigorous action break up the clay particles more quickly than will hydrated lime. Caustic lime is obtainable from a builder's

Runner beans are one of the most prized of all summer vegetables. Well-grown beans are long and straight, but it takes a rich, deep soil to produce beans as good as these. *Courtesy W. J. Unwin Ltd.*

merchant and must be kept dry. It is applied to the soil when the soil is in a reasonably dry condition, being dug well in when the moisture in the ground will cause an explosive action to take place, the clay soil disintegrating with the lime. Without lime, a heavy soil will consolidate with the winter rains and so deprive the roots of the plants of the necessary oxygen. The oxygen will also be cut off from bacteria in the soil and they will not be able to fulfil their function of converting humus into plant food.

Lime has a tendency to be washed down by rain, and where used in hydrated form it should be applied to the surface in mid-winter after the ground has been dug and the surface left in a rough condition, to be broken down by wind and frost.

The soil of town gardens which may contain heavy deposits of soot and sulphur which will contribute to its acid condition will benefit from a dressing of hydrated lime before any planting takes place for no matter how heavily the ground is manured, it will not grow good crops unless corrected for its acid condition.

A soil may also be tested for nitrogen, phosphorus and potash deficiency so that the correct requirements of each crop may be supplied and in the correct amounts, thus eliminating wastage and saving expense.

To correct nitrogen deficiency, give a 4 oz. per sq. ft. dressing with sulphate of ammonia for every 1 per cent deficiency.

To ensure the correct phosphatic content, the ground should be given a dressing of superphosphate of lime at a rate of 2 lb. per 100 sq. ft.

To correct potash deficiency, give a dressing of 2 oz. of sulphate of potash per 100 sq. ft.

If the soil shows a deficiency of each of these plant foods, a compound fertilizer may be made up to the exact requirements and applied in spring, prior to planting. Soil testing can be done quickly on the spot but as soils may differ from one part of the garden to another, it is advisable to make several tests and to make an average of soil requirements before the necessary fertilizers are obtained.

A soil testing outfit may be used over and over again, but where it is not thought necessary to obtain the outfit, the

District Horticultural Officer will usually provide a soil test and give advice on correct soil treatment.

The Value of Humus

Both light and heavy soils require humus. A clay soil so that it will open up and aerate it, to allow oxygen to penetrate to the plant roots and to assist drainage, whilst a sandy soil needs humus to bind it and to provide a moisture-holding medium during the dry summer months when plants should be making most growth but will not do so where the soil is lacking in moisture.

Humus may take the form of decayed leaves or straw that has been broken down (composted) by an activator. Peat is also useful but, being slightly acid, the soil should be given liberal dressings of lime. Peat may be used for all types of soil and so greatly improves the texture as to allow plant roots to range far and wide without restriction. Whilst it opens up a heavy soil, the spongy texture of moss peat can also be used to enable a sandy soil to hold moisture. Sphagnum moss peats are of a light brown colour and are only partially decomposed, thus being able to retain the maximum amount of moisture. They can hold up to twenty times their own weight in water. A bale of peat moss (14 bushels) will cover the surface of the ground to an area of 200 sq. ft. and to a depth of 1 in. It should be lightly forked in and is best applied in spring. To bring the soil into a condition suitable for sowing or transplanting, take up a handful and squeeze it. It will be in the correct condition if it binds together. If the soil is dry and sandy, it is advisable to moisten the peat before using it. Being almost sterile, peat is to be recommended rather than leaf-mould for with peat there is little chance of introducing either pest or disease to the soil. Poplar bark fibre may be used as an alternative but as peat and bark are almost sterile, they should be used with artificial fertilizers made to a balanced formula or with other humus-forming materials which cóntain suitable plant foods. For those living near the coast, chopped seaweed containing traces of nitrogen and potash, and for those gardening in the industrial north, wool shoddy, rich in nitrogen, will be both inexpensive and easy to use. Those living in country districts may be able to obtain some well

Savoys are the largest-heading of all cabbages, and are at their best early in the new year, when few other fresh vegetables are available. They are also the hardiest of all cabbages, and will come through the toughest winter weather without harm

decayed farmyard manure or used hops from a brewery, each supplying humus in addition to traces of the various plant foods. Old mushroom bed compost is also excellent. Where humus-forming materials are in short supply, straw composted with an activator will provide both humus and nutriment and will be easy and clean to handle.

To compost straw, obtain a bale and shake it well out in a corner of the garden, preferably where it can be surrounded with boards or corrugated iron sheeting. This will not only keep the heap tidy but will protect it from drying winds so that the straw may be more quickly composted. As the straw is spread out, soak it with water then spread a layer 12 in. deep and sprinkle over it some of the activator. Again, add more straw and more activator, building up the heap in this fashion to a height of about 5 ft. It will soon begin to heat up and in 10 days will be ready to turn, shaking out the straw and activator, giving more water if necessary and remaking the heap. Allow it to heat up for another 10 days before repeating the process and in 3 weeks the straw will have become dark brown, whilst the bits of straw will have become quite short so that they may more easily be dug into the ground.

The ultimate aim with any soil is to bring it to a fine tilth, deeply enriched with moisture-holding humus, active in bacteria and which is spongy and friable when pressed in the hands. Such a soil will be well drained yet will be moisture-retentive and will be ready to work at all times, except when covered with snow and ice. It will also warm up with the first spring sunshine so that the plants will get away to an early start.

A soil of a calcareous nature will usually have only a limited amount of top soil and whilst humus in the form of peat or garden compost will increase the depth, this may also be done by 'green' manuring. Though the high alkalinity of these soils will not be detrimental to vegetable growing, calcareous soils are usually 'hot' soils owing to their lacking depth, and in dry weather the plants dry out rapidly and make only stunted growth.

'Green' manuring is best done in early autumn. After clearing the ground of perennial weeds, it is thickly sown with rape seed. This will germinate quickly and be ready to dig into the soil during October. By then, a thick mat of fibrous roots and green top growth will have formed, and should the rape have grown tall it is cut down with shears or a scythe before digging it in to as great a depth as possible. Heavy land will also be improved by 'green' manuring and the soil should be left rough to enable the weather to improve further its structure.

Into a heavy soil, drainage materials may be incorporated at the same time, using crushed brick or mortar (with its valuable lime content), shingle or coarse sand. If the ground is low lying, an area of top-soil should be removed to a depth of 3 ft. and a base of crushed brick provided. Over this, drainage pipes should be laid of sufficient 'fall' to enable the water to be carried away to a ditch or to some other part of the garden where it will do less harm. The soil is then replaced, at the same time incorporating additional drainage and humus-forming materials.

Tomatoes out of doors. Compare this with the picture of tomatoes being grown under glass by the straw-bale method. Both pictures were taken on the same day: the indoor tomatoes have already been heavily picked

23

Organic and inorganic manures   It is not possible to grow good vegetables without the use of organic manures for these are able to supply the plant with humus in addition to nutrients, whilst valuable trace elements are also present. Those vegetables requiring a long period to mature, possibly a year or more, will need a manure which releases its plant food slowly. Farmyard manure and composted straw, material from the garden compost heap, seaweed and shoddy, are all slow-acting nitrogenous manures. Bone meal is also slow acting and has a high phosphatic value. Nitrogen is needed to make sufficient vegetation to assist in the correct functions of the plant so that it will reach its maximum size and mature correctly. Lack of nitrogen will cause the plants to be stunted and sickly, though certain crops, e.g. potatoes, can have an excess of nitrogen and the quality deteriorates, while with others, cauliflowers, for example, leaf is made at the expense of 'heart'. Thus, phosphates are required to bring the plants to full maturity whilst they also stimulate root activity. Where nitrogenous manures are being used, bone meal should accompany them especially in a lime deficient soil, or phosphates should be provided by the quick-acting fish meal or guano, both rich in nitrogen and in phosphate content. Or use superphosphate of lime which contains only phosphatic compounds, though it is a fertilizer of acid reaction which should be used only in a well-limed soil. Basic slag which has a similar phosphatic value has a high lime content and should be used in soils of acid reaction.

Nitrogen is necessary to start a plant into growth after a period of inactivity, possibly after occupying the ground over winter, or where cold winds have retarded growth. Nitrogen is given in the form of nitrate of soda which will also release pent-up potash in the soil whilst when compared to sulphate of ammonia, it does not prove so destructive to lime in the soil. Slower to release their nitrogen but less destructive to the soil are the inorganic fertilizers, soot and dried blood, both so valuable in the vegetable garden.

Potash is essential to all crops for it makes a plant grow 'hard', able to withstand adverse weather and disease. Soil deficient in potash will grow lush, soft plants which will succumb to the first frost or cold winds, or at the first sign of disease. Potash also accentuates flavour and colour. Potash may be given in the form of wood ash, which should be stored dry as both it and its potash content are readily washed away by rain. For this reason, light soils are usually devoid of potash and require replenishing with plant foods more often than heavy soils. A light soil is a hungry soil.

Fish meal, guano and poultry manure are also rich in potash but where the land is in good heart, the inorganic sulphate of potash, which has a high potash content, may be used instead, being given at planting time for it is quickly washed down to the plant's roots.

Another valuable fertilizer is liquid manure which contains a balanced diet for growing plants and is readily assimilated. It is applied through the growing season at regular intervals and may be used as a proprietary make or it may be made up to one's own requirements. This is done by half filling a sack with farmyard or poultry manure and suspending it from a stout pole placed across a galvanized tank or bin. The tank should be filled with water and the sack completely immersed. After about a fortnight, the sack is removed and the tank topped up with water. The manure water will then be ready to use, diluting it further if considered necessary. After applying to the plants it should be watered well down to the roots for best results.

Fertilizers and their food value

FERTILIZER	ACTION	NITROGEN CONTENT	PHOSPHATIC CONTENT	POTASH CONTENT
Basic Slag	Slow	15%		
Bone Meal	Slow	5%	20%	
Dried Blood	Medium	10%		
Farmyard Manure	Slow	·5%	·25%	·5%
Fish Meal	Quick	10%	8%	7%
Guano	Quick	15%	10%	7%
Kainit	Slow			13%
Nitrate of Soda	Quick	16%		
Nitro-Chalk	Quick	16%		
Potassium Nitrate	Quick	14%		40%
Poultry Manure	Medium	3%	2%	6%
Rape Meal	Slow	5%	2%	1%
Seaweed	Slow	5%		1·5%
Shoddy (Wool)	Slow	12%		
Sulphate of Ammonia	Quick	20%		
Sulphate of Potash	Medium			50%
Superphosphate	Medium		15%	
Used Hops	Slow	4%	2%	

Preparing the Ground

No amount of care in the selection and use of fertilizers and manures will be of much value unless the soil is deeply worked and cleared of all perennial weeds which would compete with the vegetables for their food and moisture.

When first bringing the ground into condition, a start should be made in autumn when the soil is still friable and is easily worked. The ground must be cleared, the soil drained and aerated, the lime content increased if need be, and brought into a friable condition by the time the first sowings are made in spring. At this stage, double digging or trenching is essential for only by working the soil two spits (spades) deep will it be possible to incorporate the necessary humus and drainage materials and to remove the deep-rooting weeds. When once the land has been deeply worked, trenching or double digging will not be necessary again, though for a number of crops trenching will be done each year to achieve best results. In this way, it is possible to concentrate the food requirements of the plants into a limited area so that they are more readily available whilst there will be less wastage.

With ground that has not been worked for some time, double digging should be done. The area should be marked out into sections of 1 sq. yd. and soil two spits deep should be taken from (A) and placed at the side of the plot (E). Soil from the next yard of ground (B) two spits deep is then moved to (A) and so on until soil at (E) is used to complete the operation by replacing that moved from section (D). Throughout the operation, the soil is treated with wireworm fumigant whilst humus and fertilizers are incorporated as the work proceeds. The ground should be left in a rough condition for the winter weather to break down to a fine tilth.

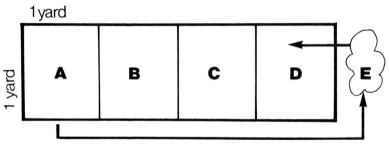

Where couch grass and other weeds difficult to eradicate have taken a hold, it is advisable to plant potatoes (though not where Gamma-BHC has been used) in spring for they are an excellent means of cleaning the ground.

The work entailed in trenching and double digging is arduous but of vital importance where good vegetable crops are to be grown. Land which has been worked to a considerable depth and contains an abundance of humus will be greatly improved in its structure. It will resemble a sponge, being divided into a multitude of soil particles each surrounded by an air space into which moisture is able to penetrate and which is held in suspension around each particle of soil. The air spaces, though reduced in volume, remain to provide the plant roots with oxygen whilst sufficient moisture will be available to support healthy plant growth, even in periods of drought. Even so, after a winter of heavy rains, the surface of the soil may have formed a crust whereby the soil particles will have 'panned' together. In order to permit air and moisture to enter, the hoe must be used to break up the surface and to suppress annual weeds. Mulching is also important, especially between rows of broad beans and other crops which will occupy the ground during winter. A mulch will not only give some protection to the plants from frost but will suppress weeds and prevent the surface of the soil from 'panning'. It will also improve soil texture by the activities of worms which will carry the particles of humus down into the ground, whilst a summer mulch will prevent the too rapid evaporation of surface moisture. If composted straw or farmyard manure is used, additional plant food will be made available which will be washed into the soil by the rains.

There are those gardeners who make so great a use of mulches that all forms of digging and other cultivations are entirely eliminated. Peat and old mushroom bed compost may be spread over the surface of the soil to a depth of 3–4 in. and this may be augmented by well decayed farmyard manure or used hops. A large worm population and bacterial activity will maintain the soil in good heart and seed is sown and plantings made without the need for any additional soil preparations. This form of cultivation is excellent on light soils, but heavy clay soils still need to be double-trenched every 6–8 years.

3 The Greenhouse and Frame

Whilst a frame will be almost as much a part of the vegetable garden as a spade, being used for hardening off seedlings and for the production of early crops, a greenhouse, though not essential, will enable a wider variety of crops to be grown. Here, crops of tomatoes and cucumbers can be produced much earlier than if relying on open air planting or on a frame and, if some form of heating is available, then out of season crops may be enjoyed.

Of numerous greenhouse types, the Dutch-light house is popular for growing tomatoes and all those crops such as winter lettuce which require the maximum amount of light. This type of house is used mostly without heat, though soil warming equipment, e.g. soil heating cables, will enable earlier crops to be grown. The house is usually constructed on a brick base of three to four courses and each light, composed of a single sheet of glass, is clipped into position, the sides having a gentle slope to allow for maximum light penetration. Made of aluminium or cedar wood, the house is quickly erected and dismantled to move elsewhere as required. The lights may also be used as frame lights if desired. No glazing is required, the lights being sent out complete and ready for erecting sectionally.

The more conventional greenhouse with a brick or wooden base extending to a height of 2 ft. and with glass sides extending for a further 3 ft. before meeting the roof will require less heat to maintain a temperature similar to that of a Dutch-light house and will enable a wider range of horticultural activities to be performed. Tomatoes and cucumbers may be grown at the back, planting them in deep boxes or pots and first training them in an upright direction, then to the top of the roof, whilst other crops may be grown at the front of the bench, or seedlings raised and cuttings rooted.

Where garden space is at a premium, the circular greenhouse is to be recommended. It is topped by a dome which lifts to provide top ventilation in addition to the all round intake of air at ground level. Instant shading is by means of spring roller blinds in green p.v.c. material which take only seconds to move up or down. Heating costs are minimized by the elimination of unnecessary headroom whilst staging provides support for plants at all levels. Heating consists of a close coiled mineral-insulated copper-sheathed cable operating at a low surface temperature and providing an all-round even distribution of heat which will raise the temperature at least 25 °F above outside temperatures.

Methods of Heating

Efficient heating is all-important when growing out-of-season crops. Violent fluctuations of temperature must be avoided whilst in case of a sharp fall in outside temperatures there should be sufficient reserve in the heating system to raise the temperature of the house to that demanded by the plants. Where raising seedlings, economies may be made by the use of a propagator which will raise the temperature to 60–70 °F to ensure rapid germination, with the minimum of expense.

To calculate the amount of heat required to raise the temperature of a conventional greenhouse to 25 °F above that of the outside temperature, the total area of base and glass must be obtained. For a house 12 ft. long and 8 ft. wide, with a 2-ft. base of brick or wood, and a door 7 ft. high, the area will be approximately 284 sq. ft. made up as follows:

2 sides with glass 12 feet × 3 feet	72 square feet
2 roof sections with glass 12 feet × 4 feet 6 inches	108 square feet
2 ends, average height of glass 8 feet × 4 feet	64 square feet
2 sides, brick 12 feet × 2 feet ÷ 2	24 square feet
2 ends, brick 8 feet × 2 feet ÷ 2	16 square feet
Total area	284 square feet

A typical half-wall greenhouse. This is the type of greenhouse that is most used in the vegetable garden

This is multiplied by ten to give the number of watts required, which to be on the safe side should be 3000.

Where electricity is available there are a number of efficient heaters on the market. Accurate thermostatic control means no wasted heat and low running costs. The heater can be instantly connected to the mains and may be allowed to stand on a wooden block or on bricks where used for heating a Dutch-light house.

It should be said that circulating air (warm in winter, cool in summer) is vital for healthy plant growth and helps to prevent botrytis, mildew and other moulds which are encouraged by a stagnant atmosphere.

Tubular heaters are also effective and may be fitted to the walls where the greenhouse has a base of wood or brick. Where wall mounting is not practical, the tubes may be held in place by spikes of galvanized iron, inserted into the ground.

Where no electric supply is available or where the house is too far from the home, a thermostatically controlled paraffin-oil-fired heater will prove invaluable to greenhouse owners.

Soil Warming

Where an electric supply is available, soil warmth for seed germination, the propagation of cuttings and for early salad crops may be inexpensively obtained by the use of warming wires and cables. A low voltage transformer unit which reduces the mains supply to a low safe voltage, is used to heat a plastic covered galvanized wire laid under a bed of soil or sand. These wires will also heat the soil in a frame used for early crops or for seed raising and where there is danger of cultivations disturbing them, warming wires should be used instead of cables. For rotational cropping, a warming wire is laid 10 in. deep in several frames and the transformer moved to each in turn, as required.

Where a hot bed cannot be made, electric soil warming is a reliable substitute, whilst for raising seedlings and striking cuttings, a sand propagating frame may be made in a cold greenhouse by using either low voltage or mains warming cables. A wooden box is made with 9-in. boards, the base being covered with felt. Over this is placed a 2-in. layer of washed sand before laying down the warming wires which are covered with a further 3-in. layer of sand on which the seed boxes or pots are stood; or cuttings (to be rooted) may be inserted directly into the sand. Eight watts per sq. ft. of bed should be allowed, whilst a soil thermostat is necessary to control the temperature of the bed.

Greenhouse Hygiene

When growing vegetable crops under glass, cleanliness is of the utmost importance. Each year, when the tomato crop is cleared in autumn, inspect the house for broken glass so that it may be replaced before the winter. It will not be possible to adequately heat a greenhouse where the warm air is continually escaping through damaged glass or where the ventilators will not close properly. Nor is it possible to fumigate efficiently for the control of pest and disease. It is usual at this time to wash the glass with warm soapy water, both inside and outside for dirty glass will prevent the sun's rays from penetrating and this is also the case with frame lights.

As a precaution against pest and disease, fumigation must

also be carried out. A simple and effective method is to burn sulphur cones or candles inside the house, either before or after the crop has been removed but sulphur should not be used where there are growing plants.

To fumigate, close up all ventilators and if the greenhouse is of some size, begin by lighting the cones or candles at the far end, and working towards the door. Sulphur fumes are irritating and must not be inhaled. Sulphur should be used at the rate of 1 lb. for every 1000 cu. ft. of air space or use one cone or candle for a house 8 ft. × 6 ft.

When the house has been fumigated, an additional precaution may be taken by passing the flame of a blow lamp over the woodwork, whilst all seed boxes and pots should be sterilized by immersing them in a tank of formalin solution, diluted to 1 part in 50 of water.

The greenhouse may be kept free from pests by the use of an aerosol which is a suspension of minute solids or liquid particles in gaseous form, thereby creating a mist which envelops each plant. The aerosol will consist of a metal container with a thermostatically controlled heating element to vaporize the liquid pesticide.

A more simple method is to fit a disc impregnated with pesticide (or fungicide) over an electric light bulb which when switched on, will release the fumigant with the heat of the bulb.

Where raising one's own plants have a supply of sterilized soil available. One method is to obtain loam of a fibrous nature and to water it with formalin solution used at a strength of 1 pt. to 10 gal. of water. As the soil is made damp, make it into a heap 2–3 ft. high and cover with a tarpaulin or plastic sheeting to retain the fumes. Leave for a week, then remove the cover to allow the soil to be turned for the fumes to escape. It should be turned several more times until quite free of any fumes. This will take about a month when it may be used.

Electric soil sterilizers are most efficient and will sterilize a bushel of soil at one time and are automatically controlled, switching off after sterilization is complete.

After the soil has been sterilized, the various John Innes composts may be made up according to the proven formula but they should not be made up before the soil has been sterilized.

4 Raising plants

Upon the successful raising of the plants, the crop will depend. Vegetables are raised by several methods:

(i)   By sowing under glass in a propagator or in a warm greenhouse.

(ii) By sowing over a hot bed in a frame, in an unheated frame or greenhouse, or under cloches.

(iii) By sowing directly into the open ground.

Those plants requiring a long growing season to mature or where an early crop is to be raised such as tomatoes or cucumbers under glass, sowing in a heated greenhouse will be necessary, but where only small numbers of plants are needed, a simple propagating unit will be more economical to use. It may be placed in a garden room or greenhouse and run from the electricity supply. In a propagator, plants may be raised from seed which may prove difficult to germinate without heat. There are a number of efficient propagators on the market.

Sowing Seed Indoors

Seeds are sown in boxes or pans but for those plants which do not transplant readily, seeds should be sown in $\frac{1}{2}$-in. cubes made of specially prepared plant food. After germination, the cubes are planted (just as they are) in peat pots and the plants grown on in a reduced temperature.

Preparing a seed box. (i) The bottom of the box is covered with coarse peat to provide drainage. (ii) Next the growing compost is added. (iii) Then the seeds are planted. (iv) The seeds are then covered to the right depth and firmed with a flat piece of wood

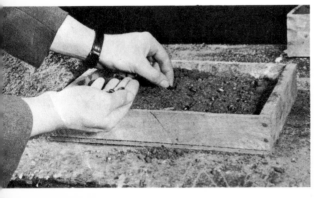

Hotbeds are still the finest way of raising many crops including tomatoes, cucumbers and other tender vegetables. The diagram shows how the frame should be placed on top of the hot-bed

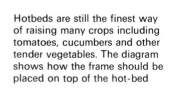

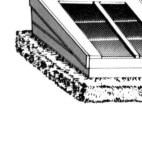

Where sowing in boxes or pans, sow thinly or space out the seeds to an inch apart to allow the seedlings room to develop. Overcrowding at this stage will result in a drawn, 'leggy' plant which will never recover. Obtain the best seed from growers with a reputation to maintain. It will cost rather more but will amply repay its cost in reliable germination.

Sowing composts may vary slightly, but as a general rule the John Innes compost is to be recommended. It may be purchased from most garden stores but should be in a fresh condition. If made up for any length of time it may have become contaminated with disease spores while the superphosphate used in its formula and so valuable in promoting vigorous root action, will have lost its strength. The John Innes compost is made up of:

2 parts loam (sterilized)
1 part peat
1 part sand } *per bushel*
$1\frac{1}{2}$ oz. superphosphate
$\frac{3}{4}$ oz. ground limestone

The compost should be in a moist, friable condition, and after sowing the seeds are lightly covered with additional compost and watered in before placing in the propagator.

After germination, transplant the seedlings into boxes or pots containing the John Innes potting compost:

7 parts loam (sterilized)
3 parts peat
2 parts sand } *per bushel*
$\frac{3}{4}$ oz. ground limestone
$\frac{1}{2}$ lb. John Innes Base

The John Innes Base is made up of:

2 parts Hoof and Horn meal
2 parts superphosphate
1 part sulphate of potash

If making up one's own composts, do not exceed the amounts stated for it has been established that seedlings grow better in a slightly acid compost than in one of an alkaline nature.

Soil-less composts, composed mainly of peat and sand with

added nutrients are less heavy to handle but require considerably more care with their watering for they dry out rapidly. Experience is needed in their use for best results.

It is important that where raising seedlings in a propagator or in a heated greenhouse, there is no undue delay in their transplanting, otherwise they will have used up the nutrients in their sowing compost and will grow hard and woody. The roots will be brown instead of white, the foliage yellow instead of green.

If the seed has been sown early in the year, it will be necessary to maintain a temperature of around 60 °F by day in greenhouse or frame, the latter being heated by soil wires or cables. The plants must be kept growing on without check and if correct conditions cannot be provided, it will be better to buy in one's plants from a reputable supplier at the appropriate time.

Transplanting

To transplant, have the boxes or pots already filled with the J.I. potting compost and, holding the plant with the fingers of one hand, carefully loosen the roots with a piece of smooth-ended wood or cane held in the other hand. Then lift from the compost with one movement and transfer the plant to the new growing medium, inserting the roots and making quite firm. Make sure that the plants have room to develop. Water in and maintain a humid but not a stuffy atmosphere. Those plants which resent root disturbance may be grown on in soil blocks made to the formula of the J.I. potting compost, or in Jiffy pots. These are made from 75 per cent wood pulp impregnated with essential nutrients and are made round or square and 3 in. in diameter. If using boxes or clay pots, make sure they have been scrubbed clean before use. When ready to move to larger pots or when planting out, the plants are removed with the soil ball intact or each compartment may be detached and sold without disturbing the roots.

Cauliflowers and other plants raised in a warm greenhouse may be removed to a cold frame by April 1st for hardening and planting out at the month end. By then, the plants should be about 4 in. tall, sturdy and bright green. They should be in the same condition if purchased from a garden shop or nurseryman. If yellowish green and too tall (drawn), this will signify that the plants have been sown too soon or may have been raised in too warm a temperature. Again, they may not have been hardened.

Early crops and plants set out in the open may be raised in frames by sowing direct into a prepared seed bed which has been brought to a fine tilth and into which peat or old mushroom bed compost has been incorporated. Vegetable plants should be sown early in March, and after hardening may be planted out in April. In the more favourable parts of the south and west seed is sown a month earlier in frames (or under cloches) and the plants set out about April 1st; or a sowing may be made directly into the open ground early in March. For an early crop of frame cucumbers or marrows, seed is sown in spring over a hot bed made in a frame. This is made by composting straw, or from farmyard manure. Additional heat will be obtained if some poultry manure is added to the straw during composting. Straw will take about three weeks to compost and should be placed in the frame to a depth of about 15 in. and covered with 5–6 in. of soil to prevent loss of heat. When the temperature has fallen to 80 °F, the seed is sown in the soil or in pots inserted into the soil. The frame is kept closed to maintain a humid condition and hasten germination. A mild hot bed may be used for a crop of early turnips, radishes or carrots which will be sweet and succulent. Afterwards, the compost may be used on the land.

Sowing in the Open

Vegetables may also be grown entirely without any form of heat and without the use of a frame though a row of cloches will ensure earlier crops and they may be kept in use the whole year round. Cloches are like small portable greenhouses and are of many types and sizes. The barn-type is made of glass sheets, held together by galvanized wires. Being 19 in. high it is suitable for melons and marrows, tomatoes and cucumbers until they reach maturity. It is ideal for strawberries too. Low barn cloches are 12 in. high and are suitable for growing winter lettuce and early crops of turnips, radishes and beetroot. They may also be used to cover rows of early spring-sown

Left to right (i) Preparing the seed bed. The surface should be worked to a fine tilth with a rake, using the back of the rack to break up any large lumps. (ii) A line is inserted in the ground. (iii) A shallow trench is taken out with a hoe.

seedlings. Later, the plants are hardened by removing the cloches on mild days and then at night, when the plants will be ready to transplant during April.

Cloches made of strong p.v.c. sheets held in place by wire hoops which skewer firmly into the ground, are unbreakable and light to handle, whilst an inexpensive tunnel cloche, 35 ft. long may be made from polythene sheeting supported by hoops and securing wires. Where growing under cloches, cover the ground several days before the seed is sown so that the soil is partially warm at sowing time which will ensure more rapid germination.

Always sow thinly, using pelleted seed where possible for pelleting makes small seeds easier to handle and to sow, while correct spacing does away with much labour in thinning and allows the plants space to develop properly. Pelleted seeds are dried to a low moisture level which causes the coating to break down more quickly.

Seeds for transplanting may be sown in drills or broadcast in prepared beds. First make the soil friable by breaking down all lumps and incorporate into the top 3–4 in. some moist peat or bark fibre and give a sprinkling of superphosphate to encourage root action. When the soil is in a reasonably dry, friable condition, the drills are made 1 in. deep with the back

(iv) The seed is sown. (v) The trench is filled in, covering with seed, with a rake. (vi) The row is then labelled clearly with the name of the seed and the date on which it was sown. Ideally the row should be labelled at both ends

of a rake. Use a line to make them straight and if the rows are to be covered with cloches, make them of the correct width.

With crops which are to be grown on to maturity under cloches, the seedlings need thinning to the correct distances apart and they will require attention as to their watering, though in showery weather sufficient moisture will percolate under each side of the cloches and it will be necessary to move them only occasionally. If strips of black polythene are placed between the rows, they will attract and retain the warmth of the sun's rays and this will make for earlier maturity as well as suppressing weeds and reducing moisture evaporation from the soil.

Planting Out

Thinning should be done with care, removing any plants where there is overcrowding and any weakly or diseased plants. After thinning, gently make firm those plants remaining. To transplant, lift when the soil is damp and with as much soil attached to the roots as possible. Brassicas should have the roots dipped in calomel solution before replanting. Do not lift more plants than can be handled in a reasonably short time for if the roots are long exposed to sun and wind, flagging may occur from which they may take some time to recover. If possible, plant on a dull day. Plant firmly, using a trowel and insert the roots well into the ground. Between the rows, crops of radishes and lettuce may be grown which will have reached maturity long before the cabbages and cauliflowers have become fully grown. Keep the plants growing during dry weather by giving the soil around the roots a thorough soaking. This is important for if only surface waterings are given, the roots will turn upwards in search of moisture and will not only suffer harm from exposure to the sun and drying winds but the plants will lack the nutrition and moisture essential for their full maturity.

After planting, keep a close look out for pests and disease and use the spray at the first appearance. For a small garden, the ASL Cadet spray is to be recommended. It has a 4-pt. capacity and gives 7 min. of continuous spraying. It is fitted with a thumb control tap and a long reach extension arm. This model may also be used for spraying roses and fruit trees.

At all times keep the hoe moving between the plants to prevent the appearance of weeds and to keep the surface broken up so that air and moisture may penetrate to the roots.

Hoeing may be eliminated by mulching between the plants but apart from peat, mulching materials are expensive and difficult to obtain, though composted straw will serve the purpose. A mulch will suppress weeds and prevent too rapid moisture evaporation of the soil whilst certain mulches provide valuable plant food. They should be applied when the soil has warmed, about midsummer. If peat is used in quantity, additional liming may be necessary for future crops.

As they come to maturity, plants will benefit from a weekly application of dilute manure water whilst those which are making less growth than expected, possibly because of cold winds and a soil slow to warm, should be stimulated by giving a dressing of nitrate of soda, a quick acting fertilizer with a high nitrogen content. The plants will also benefit from weathered soot which, if applied early in summer, will encourage the soil to warm up and will also provide additional nitrogen.

During dry periods, all plants will appreciate a syringeing of the foliage, given in the evening when the sun is going down.

Earthing up will also help the taller growing plants to

resist strong winds whilst leeks and celery will require earthing up at regular intervals for their satisfactory blanching, and potatoes to prevent the haulm being broken away during cultivations.

Vegetables do need some attention to get the best from them and particularly is it important to harvest them whilst still young and full of flavour. Nothing is gained by allowing them to remain too long on the plants so that they run to seed or grow too large with the resultant loss of flavour and quality. In addition, if removed when young, others are able to come to maturity and each plant will yield its maximum crop and cropping will last over a longer period.

When to sow

VEGETABLE	MONTH	DEPTH
Artichoke, Globe	March, August	1 inch
Bean, broad	October, March	2 inches
Bean, dwarf	May	2 inches
Bean, runner	May	3 inches
Beetroot	April–May	1 inch
Broccoli	March	1 inch
Brussels sprouts	March	1 inch
Cabbage (spring)	July	1 inch
Cabbage (winter)	April–May	1 inch
Cabbage, Chinese	April	1 inch
Cabbage, Red	September	1 inch
Carrot (maincrop)	April	$\frac{1}{2}$ inch
Cauliflower (early)	September	1 inch
Cauliflower (late)	March	1 inch
Celery	March	$\frac{1}{2}$ inch
Chicory	June	1 inch
Cucumber (frame)*	March–April	1–2 inches
Cucumber (indoors)*	March	1–2 inches
Cucumber (ridge)	March	1–2 inches
Endive	July–August	1 inch
Kohl Rabi	April–July	1 inch
Leek	March	$\frac{1}{2}$ inch
Lettuce (outdoors)	March–June	Just cover
Lettuce (indoors)	September	Just cover
Marrow	March–April	1 inch
Onion	September, February	1 inch
Onion, spring	August, March	$\frac{1}{2}$ inch
Orach	April–September	1 inch
Parsnip	March	$\frac{1}{2}$ inch
Pea (early)	November	2 inches
Pea (mid-season)	March	2 inches
Pea (late)	April–May	2 inches
Radish	March–July	$\frac{1}{2}$ inch
Rutabaga (Swede)	May	1 inch
Savoy	March–April	1 inch
Spinach	March–July	1 inch
Sweet Corn	March	2 inches
Tomato*	January	1 inch
Turnip	March–June	1 inch

*Sow under glass

Planting distances

VEGETABLE	MONTH	DISTANCE APART IN ROWS	BETWEEN ROWS
Artichoke, Globe	April	3 feet	3 feet
Artichoke, Jerusalem	March	12 inches	2 feet
Bean, broad	March–April	8 inches	9 inches
Bean, dwarf	May–June	8 inches	12 inches
Bean, runner	May	9 inches	10–12 inches
Beetroot	May	6–8 inches	15 inches
Broccoli	April–July	2 feet	2 feet
Brussels sprouts	April	2 feet	2 feet
Cabbage (spring)	September	16 inches	18 inches
Cabbage (winter)	April–May	20 inches	24 inches
Cabbage, Chinese	July	9 inches	12 inches
Cabbage, Red	March	2 feet	2 feet
Cauliflower (early)	October	20 inches	2 feet
Cauliflower (late)	April–May	2 feet	2 feet
Celery	June	10–12 inches	12 inches
Chicory	June	10 inches	18 inches
Cucumber (frame)	April–May	3 feet	
Cucumber (indoors)	March–April	3 feet	
Cucumber (ridge)	June	3 feet	
Garlic	October, March	6 inches	12 inches
Kohl Rabi	May, July	9 inches	15 inches
Leek	May, June	9 inches	6 inches
Lettuce (outdoors)	April–July	9 inches	12 inches
Lettuce (indoors)	October	6 inches	6–8 inches
Marrow (Bush)	June	3–4 feet	
Marrow (Trailing)	June	5–6 feet	
Onion	April	6 inches	12 inches
Parsnip	March	10 inches	18 inches
Pea (early)	November	3 inches	18 inches
Pea (mid-season)	March	3 inches	2 feet 6 inches
Pea (late)	April–May	3 inches	3 feet
Potato	April–May	9–10 inches	2 feet
Rutabaga (Swede)	May	9 inches	18 inches
Savoy	April–May	2 feet	2 feet
Seakale	March–April	16 inches	16 inches
Shallot	March–April	10 inches	10 inches
Sweet Corn	June	15 inches	15 inches
Tomato (indoors)	January–April	2 feet	2 feet
Tomato (outdoors)	June	2 feet	2 feet

All the vegetables and herbs shown here can be grown by the keen gardener. With a little ingenuity he can keep the family supplied with all the fresh vegetables they can eat

PART II
EASILY
GROWN
VEGETABLES

Bean, Broad *Vicia faba*

Broad beans bridge the gap in the kitchen garden between the late spring greens and the first of the summer crops and with their rich earthy flavour are welcome at this time. They are appetizing when steamed until tender and served with parsley sauce.

Sowing They like a deeply worked soil, and one which has been manured for a previous crop. If it has not been, work into the soil some well decayed manure or old mushroom bed compost. They like an alkaline soil, one which has been well limed.

In a sheltered garden, a sowing may be made early November and left unprotected during winter. When gardening in colder parts, it is advisable to cover the young plants with cloches during severe weather. A second sowing is made early March to mature later.

Sow in a double row 9 in. apart, so that both rows may be covered by a barn cloche. Allow the same distance between the beans in the rows. Plant the seeds singly, about 2 in. deep. It is preferable to use a trowel rather than a dibber because the seeds are large and if the hole is not made large enough, the seeds may be held against the sides. If the soil is heavy, it is advisable to assist winter drainage by planting on a layer of peat or sand.

General cultivation When the plants begin to make growth in spring, hoe between the rows and earth up the base of the plants. If the garden is exposed, support the plants by placing canes along the rows at regular intervals on each side of the plants and fasten twine about 12 in. above soil level and again

Diagram of a frame for growing runner beans. Now that pea sticks are becoming scarce, more and more people are trying alternatives. This is one of the best, since the beans hang downwards and outwards, making harvesting easy

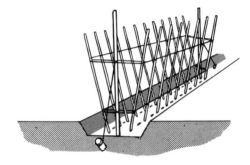

when the plants are about 2 ft. tall. Support may also be given by inserting short branches into the soil between the rows and on the outer sides. This is done when the plants are about 2 in. tall. The 'Longpod' varieties are the hardiest and most prolific; the 'Windsors' have the best flavour but should be sown only in spring.

PESTS AND DISEASES

BLACK FLY   This is the most troublesome for the broad bean. It attacks the blossom causing deformed beans and reduces the crop. It rarely attacks autumn sown plants and as it normally congregates at the top of the plant, if this is pinched out early in spring when a fair crop has set, this will greatly discourage the pest. This will also make for early maturity of the pods. The pest may also be kept under control by spraying the plants from mid-April with derris solution.

CHOCOLATE SPOT   This occurs as light brown spots on the leaves and stems which, if not controlled, may cause the plants to die back. The disease is most prevalent in a cold, wet spring and in a soil deficient in potash. Spraying with Bordeaux Mixture will give control.

VARIETIES

'BUNYARD'S EXHIBITION'   One of the best long-pods, being the first to mature from a late autumn sowing. The pale green seeds are of delicate flavour.

'LONGFELLOW'   This has received an Award of Merit and is one of the finest all-round broad beans ever introduced. It has tremendous cropping powers whilst the long straight pods contain 8–9 beans.

'PROLIFIC LONGPOD'   One of the best maincrop beans for general cultivation, bred to give the heaviest possible crop of medium-sized pods of excellent flavour. Reliable in all districts: good on heavy soils.

45

'THE MIDGET' Also known as 'Dwarf Bush', it grows only 15 in. high and each plant produces 3–4 stems, each bearing a cluster of beans up to 6 in. long. It is best planted as a single row as each plant grows 18 in. across. It does well in poor soils.

Bean, dwarf French *Phaseolus vulgaris*

One of the most prized of summer vegetables, it is suitable for growing in the smallest of gardens, and in tubs or window boxes where there is no garden. Dwarf, or Bush beans as they are called will provide a succession of food from June (or earlier where grown under glass) until autumn and will yield a larger amount of edible green for the ground they occupy than any other crop. Neither do they require staking. Native of North Africa, they are tender and unless sown in a frame or beneath cloches, should not be planted out in the more exposed parts until May so that when the seed germinates, there will be no fear of frost damage.

The plant requires a light, warm soil and an open, sunny situation. As for all legumes, lime is an essential part of their diet and 4 oz. per sq. yd. should be applied to the soil during winter. The soil, too, must be friable and well drained and contain plenty of humus such as hops, cow manure or oil mushroom bed compost. The plants will begin to crop within eight weeks of the seed being sown and will continue to bear for the same length of time. The seed may be sown between rows of lettuce or cabbage or on soil thrown up from celery trenches and which will not be used for earthing up until the beans have finished cropping.

Sowing the seed The first sowing, under cloches, is made in March, though plants raised in gentle heat and set out under cloches towards the month end will give more reliable results. Beans transplant well and it is usual to sow seeds under cloches or in a frame to fill in any spaces in the row which may occur with outdoor sowings, the first being made about mid-April in the south, a fortnight later in the north and at monthly intervals until mid-July, to give a succession of beans until the end of September. For early sowings use a quick maturing variety such as 'Earligreen' or 'The Prince' and plant with a

46

Dwarf French beans are ideal for smaller gardens and do not need staking. They produce very heavy crops of excellent flavour

trowel, 2 in. deep and 8 in. apart in the rows. If sowing a double row, plant 12 in. apart and stagger the planting to allow each room to develop. Or plant the seeds 4 in. apart and remove alternate plants when large enough to handle, transplanting them into nearby ground. After germination, keep the hoe moving between the rows and tread in any plants blown over by strong winds. In dry weather, water copiously, otherwise the beans will grow hard and stringy, and to prolong the crop, give an occasional application with dilute manure water.

Care is necessary when picking the crop so as not to loosen the roots of the plants when removing the beans, which should be harvested whilst young and succulent. If allowed to remain too long on the plants they will deteriorate both in quality and flavour, whilst the total weight of the crop will be greatly reduced. They mature rapidly and from early July it is advisable to look over the plants daily. The beans should break with a snap when pressed, hence their name 'snap' beans.

PESTS AND DISEASES

ANTHRACNOSE   The. beans may become infected by dark brown sunken spots scattered over the pod which will eventually damage the seeds. The disease rarely attacks outdoor plants except in damp humid seasons. If observed, spray the plants up to flowering time with half strength Bordeaux Mixture.

BLACK FLY   This aphis will occasionally trouble the dwarf bean but may be controlled by dusting the plants with derris powder as for broad beans.

HALO BLIGHT   A bacterial seed-borne disease which will produce a stunted or yellow plant which soon dies. It appears on all parts of the plant as pale brown spots with a transparent halo-like margin from which may ooze a slimy liquid. Spraying with weak Bordeaux Mixture gives control.

VARIETIES

'DUPLEX'   Noted for its heavy cropping and resistance to all diseases. The beans are long and are entirely stringless, whilst the flavour is all that could be desired.

'EARLIGREEN'   The first to mature, often coming into bearing 10 days before any other variety. Of compact habit, it bears long straight pods, often 6 in. long, which are fleshy and easy to slice.

'MASTERPIECE'   Probably the best dwarf bean ever introduced, cropping abundantly, the long green pods being of crispy texture and of delicious flavour.

'THE PRINCE'   With its long thin pods of brilliant green, crisp and stringless, it is outstanding for exhibition. The pods often measure up to 12 in. long.

Bean, French climbing *Phaseolus vulgaris*

Also known as the Pole bean, this combines the delicate flavour of the French varieties with the heavy cropping of the runner beans. They may be grown against trellis or netting as for runners or against a sunny wall. They may also be grown up twiggy branches 5–6 ft. tall and made to form a hedge, like sweet peas.

Sow in April 12 in. apart and nip out the growing point when the plants are 6 in. tall. This will encourage the side shoots to form. Plants may also be raised in small pots under glass for planting out in May, or they may be grown entirely under glass and brought into bearing in a temperature of 60 °F. Sow one seed to a 6-in. pot containing an open, friable soil enriched with some decayed manure. Grow them up 4-ft. canes and stop the plants when 6 in. tall and again when they reach the top of the canes. Spray during warm weather and keep the compost moist.

VARIETIES

'AMATEUR'S PRIDE'   This is a climbing form of 'The Prince', possessing all its good points and bearing even more heavily over many weeks.

'BLUE COCO'   A climbing bean, the flowers, stems and pods being of purple-blue and with a flavour surpassing all others. Of rapid growth, it matures early and continues to crop for 10–12 weeks.

Bean, Runner *Phaseolus coccineus*

Runner or kidney beans follow French beans, being at their best during late summer and autumn. The runners are more demanding as to their culture for they will reach a height of 8–10 ft. in a single season and are in every way heavier than other climbing beans. They require a rich soil and efficient staking, and are best grown against rows of laths which have one end inserted into the ground and the other held in position by strong wire or twine fastened to stout stakes at each end of the row.

The ground should be trenched where the plants are to grow and before fixing the laths in position. The trench is made 10 in. deep and to the width of a spade and at the bottom is placed material from the compost heap which is limed and well trodden down. Over this is spread a layer of soil and decayed manure. The trench being filled up with sifted soil to which is added 1 oz. of superphosphate and $\frac{1}{2}$ oz. of sulphate of potash per yard of trench.

Insert the stakes at intervals of 9 in. and tie in place to a stout wire stretched 4–5 ft. above the trench. Canes may be used instead of laths but the plants prefer to twine about rough laths and this way pull themselves up more quickly.

One seed is planted at the foot of each stake, planting the seed 3 in. deep. It is usual to set a dozen or so seeds at the end of the row to fill in any 'misses'. Mid-May is the best time to plant for runner beans will be damaged by frost if they appear above ground before June 1st.

General cultivation As soon as the plants begin to form their first beans, they should receive an application of dilute liquid manure once each week until early in August; they will also benefit from a mulch of strawy manure. Above all, the plants must not be allowed to suffer from lack of moisture at the roots, otherwise the buds and beans may fall and the older beans will mature tough and stringy. Regular spraying of the foliage will help the flowers to set and will keep the plants free from red spider. When the plants reach to the top of the stakes it is advisable to remove the growing points so that they may concentrate their energies on the production of beans rather than in making more growth.

Where space is limited, runners may be grown against stakes fixed in tent fashion and tied at the top, with the bottom of the stakes 2 ft. apart. Though no trenching will be done, the soil should be made rich and friable before planting the seed. Dwarf runner beans, supported by twiggy sticks and started under cloches will also crop heavily in a confined space.

Runner beans suffer from neither pest nor disease which cannot be prevented by the normal precautionary methods.

Slugs must be guarded against and red spider, by frequently syringeing the foliage during dry weather or if growing close to a wall. It is possibly the most trouble-free of all crops.

VARIETIES

'CRUSADER'   An exhibitor's favourite for its beans will grow 18 in. long yet remain straight and slim. It also does well in all soils and in all weathers and does not drop its buds at the least provocation. Also excellent for the table.

'HAMMOND'S DWARF'   A dwarf form of the long established 'Prizewinner' and growing only 18 in. tall. The 8-in. long pods are produced over a period of 10–12 weeks and are tender and sweet if not left on the plant too long. It may be grown under barn cloches for an early crop, the seed being sown late in April and the cloches removed mid-June.

'STREAMLINE'   An outstanding exhibitor's bean. The 18-in. long pods grow straight and slim, whilst they are borne in large trusses right through the season.

Beetroot   *Beta vulgaris*

There is now a golden beetroot to add to the ever popular red varieties and which is a valuable dual-purpose vegetable for the tops may be screwed off and cooked like spinach whilst the

Beetroot needs a deep, stone-free soil to do really well. Good drainage is essential, as too much moisture can make them split

roots are boiled and used in salads when cold. Or they may be preserved in malt vinegar to be used when required.

Beetroot is a maritime plant, requiring a sandy soil and one containing some salt. Before sowing the seed, dress the ground with 1 oz. per sq. yd. of common salt and the same amount of superphosphate and sulphate of potash mixed together.

Sowing Seed is sown about mid-April in the south; early May in the north – for the young plants may be harmed by frost if they appear too early. Sow in drills 1 in. deep and 15 in. apart. An ounce of seed will sow a 30-yd. row.

Beet seed is now packeted in pelleted form whereby each seed is covered with a coating of plant food. This gives protection from disease whilst germinating. The coating is pre-programmed to break down quickly when sowing has taken place.

Pelleted seeds are more easily sown individually and may be spaced at distances which will later avoid the need for thinning, thus saving time, energy and money.

Beet is best grown in a friable soil which has been manured for a previous crop. If not, work in some peat or leaf-mould, together with a small amount of decayed manure. Old mushroom bed compost is ideal whilst anything of an organic nature may be dug in to lighten the soil and to help to retain summer moisture. This is a crop that must never lack water or the roots will grow coarse and 'woody', whilst the plants will run to seed prematurely in warm weather if deprived of moisture.

As the roots make growth, remove alternate plants when reaching tennis ball size, to use in summer salads after boiling. This will allow the remaining roots to grow on to a larger size for winter use.

The plants will benefit from a $\frac{1}{2}$ oz. per sq. yd. dressing of common salt given in July, preferably during showery weather.

A second sowing may be made during June to provide additional roots for winter storage.

Harvesting When lifting, care must be taken to ensure that the roots are not in any way damaged, for with many varieties the smallest cut or bruising of the skin will cause the roots to 'bleed' so that, when pickled, they will turn pink and will have lost much of their flavour.

Lift the roots in October, before the frosts, and while the soil is still dry and friable. Always twist away the leaves rather than cut them off with a knife, for twisting will reduce bleeding to a minimum. Then place the roots in boxes of dry sand or peat in a frost-proof room for use as required.

PESTS AND DISEASES

DOWNY MILDEW   This occasionally troubles beetroot, appearing as a white powder on the underside of the leaves. It may be controlled by spraying the seedling plants with a weak solution of Bordeaux Mixture.

PHOMA LINGHAM   This causes young beet seedlings to turn brown and decay. It is a seed-borne disease, for which reason seedsmen now market Thiram-soaked seed which will guard against an outbreak.

VARIETIES

'AVON EARLY'   The best beet to sow early for it does not readily 'bolt' whilst it produces roots of uniformly good size and shape and of good colouring.

'BURPEE'S GOLDEN'   Introduced in 1970, it is an entirely new colour break and is a vegetable of the first importance for exhibition and culinary use. The roots develop rapidly and are ready to use within 60 days of sowing, the skin being deep golden-yellow whilst the flesh has a mild, sweet flavour. There is no 'bleeding' as with most of the red varieties.

'DETROIT GLOBE'   An old favourite and possibly the best all-round beet ever introduced. Perfectly globular, the skin is deepest crimson, the flesh free from any paler 'rings' when cooked. The flesh is crisp and sweet.

Broccoli, Large-heading   *Brassica oleracea*

There are two forms, the large-heading (winter cauliflower) and the sprouting, both valuable crops for winter and spring use, though by planting several varieties or strains it will be possible to bring the large-heading varieties to maturity almost throughout the year.

53

To withstand a severe winter, the large-heading must be grown well from sowing time. As the plants take 12 months to reach maturity, those required for March cutting should be sown the previous March; those to be cut in May being sown the May before and so on. It is therefore necessary to obtain a strain sufficiently hardy to withstand the type of winter experienced in that part of the country where they are to be grown.

Sowing   Seed is sown in a frame or in prepared outdoor beds and, to have a sturdy plant capable of withstanding a hard winter, over-crowding must be prevented. Sow thinly and remove any seedlings at an early date after germination, should they appear to be growing too closely.

Seed may also be sown in shallow drills made with the back of a rake, and here again thin sowing is desirable, thinning out if necessary. In this way, transplanting is not done, the plants being set out into the open ground when large enough to move. If raising plants in boxes under glass or over a hot bed, transplanting into boxes or frames will be necessary.

Requiring a long season to mature means that the plants must receive sufficient nourishment to form large heads and this should be made available over a long period. At the same time, an excess of nitrogen will cause the plants to grow 'soft' and they may be damaged by frost and cold winds.

Planting   If possible, plant in a well drained soil which has been manured for a previous crop and augmented by a 2 oz. per sq. yd. dressing of hoof and horn meal given just prior to planting. Where growing in land which has not been previously manured, work in a slow-acting nitrogenous fertilizer such as shoddy or decayed manure, supplemented by a dressing of bone meal whilst, to build up a 'hard' plant, work into the soil 1 oz. per sq. yd. of sulphate of potash given at planting time.

As with sprouts, firm ground is essential for the formation of a tight head. Set out the plants 2 ft. apart and insert the roots well into the ground, making the soil quite firm. Planting should be done during showery weather but not when the soil is sticky. Late spring and early summer is the usual time, those late to mature being planted out in July.

After planting, keep the hoe moving along the rows and

water copiously during periods of drought. Should the weather be unduly severe in winter, the heads may be protected by bending over them the long leaves which surround them. This is done by breaking the mid-rib at a point level with the top of the curd. This will also keep the head clean.

The heads are cut as soon as they reach maturity before they begin to go to seed.

PESTS AND DISEASES

CABBAGE CATERPILLAR   It is the grub of the Cabbage White butterfly which lays its eggs on the brassicas and in a few days small cream coloured grubs hatch out. They devour the leaves and penetrate to the centre of the head. They are eradicated only by immersing the head in salt water for an hour before cooking. To control, dust the plants with derris powder once a fortnight from early June until September.

CLUB ROOT   Also known as 'Finger and Toe', it attacks all the brassicas, the roots becoming swollen and knobbly. It is caused by a slime fungus which lives on decayed vegetable matter in the soil. Well limed land which is adequately drained will rarely support the disease but, as a further precaution, dust the roots of all brassicas with calomel before planting.

DAMPING OFF   This is due to a water-borne fungus and affects seedlings at an early stage, causing them to turn black, wilt and die back. It chiefly attacks the roots and stems at soil level. As it may be present in soils which have not been sterilized, and as there is no known cure, it must be prevented by watering the soil with Cheshunt Compound when the seeds are sown.

VARIETIES

'EARLY PENZANCE'   Maturing late in autumn, it is the first variety to cut, forming firm white heads of medium size (autumn).

'KNIGHT'S PROTECTING' Hardy and self-protecting, it is possibly the best April-maturing broccoli for the home grower. It forms a solid head of purest white.

'LEAMINGTON' A top quality broccoli of proven merit for cutting April and May, the heads being large and of firm texture.

'ROYAL OAK' This makes a dwarf compact plant and matures early in June, the pure white heads remaining firm in the hottest weather.

Broccoli, Sprouting *Brassica oleracea*

For the home grower, there is no more valuable plant, for both the white and purple-sprouting varieties possess extreme hardiness and may be grown anywhere in the British Isles to provide a succession of shoots for boiling or braising from early spring until the end of summer. It comes into full cropping when the equally hardy Brussels sprout is finishing.

As the sprouting broccoli grows tall it should be given protection from strong winds and, as it is semi-perennial, it will occupy the ground for several years.

General cultivation With its continuous cropping, sprouting broccoli requires a rich, deeply worked soil, into which decayed manure, garden compost or shoddy has been incorporated. The plants will also appreciate during winter a mulch of strawy manure which should be forked in around the plants early in spring.

From an April sowing, the seedlings will be ready to plant out 3 ft. apart, in May. As with sprouts, firm planting is essential, otherwise the mature plants may be blown over by strong winds. As they make growth, the soil around them should be trodden firm.

The shoots are removed when young, whilst they are tender and mild of flavour. If left ungathered, they will run to seed, especially in warm weather when they will not only be useless for cooking but will rapidly exhaust the plant. If the shoots are continually removed, others will take their place.

VARIETIES

'EARLY PURPLE SPROUTING' From a March sowing, there will be a regular supply of purple shoots from Christmas onwards.

'NINE STAR PERENNIAL' One of the most useful of all vegetables for, with good cultivation, it will continue to produce its small cauliflower shoots almost indefinitely, coming into bearing in March each year and producing eight or nine heads from each plant during spring and summer. To maintain productivity, the plants should be given a liberal dressing of nitrogenous manure each winter.

Brussels Sprouts *Brassica oleracea*

The most important of winter vegetables for it begins to crop in October and continues until March, spanning the six coldest months of the year. It is extremely hardy and will continue to bear sprouts no matter how severe the weather.

To have firm sprouts which retain their shape after cooking, the plants must be grown well. They should be sturdy and compact and be grown in firm ground. A long jointed plant growing in loose soil will produce a large, open sprout which is not required.

Brussel sprouts are the most important of all winter vegetables. They will continue cropping well through the most severe weather. To be grown well they need a firm soil that is not too rich

57

For those who don't have either the time or the space to raise all their own vegetables from seed, garden centres are invaluable. These are seedling sprouts ready to plant out. *Courtesy W. J. Unwin Ltd.*

Sowing Brussels sprouts require a long season, so make two sowings, one about September 1st to come into bearing in the autumn of the following year and another in March to crop during the latter weeks of the following winter and through spring.

If the seed is sown thinly in a frame or in drills, transplanting will not be necessary.

As they crop over a long period, a rich well prepared soil is necessary, one which has been worked in winter and has been given a dressing of lime. The soil should be allowed to 'weather' and in spring, when free from frost, work in some well composted strawy manure or wool shoddy, both of which will release their nitrogen steadily and over a long period. Just before planting, fork in 4 oz. per sq. yd. of hoof or horn meal and 2 oz. per sq. yd. of superphosphate and sulphate of potash mixed together. This will help both to build up a sturdy plant and with the formation of hard, crisp sprouts.

General cultivation   Plant early in April 2–3 ft. apart and make the soil firm about the roots.

After planting keep the hoe moving between the rows and tread the soil around the roots so that when in bearing the heavily weighted plants will not blow over. A late summer mulch of strawy manure will assist the plants in their cropping.

Early in autumn, remove any decayed leaves and begin to harvest the sprouts before they become large and coarse. If they do, they will lose flavour and will prevent the later forming sprouts from reaching maturity. To remove the sprouts, snap them from the main stem, gathering one or two from each plant as they reach about an inch in diameter.

PESTS AND DISEASES

CABBAGE ROOT FLY   This is the most serious pest attacking Brussels sprouts and all brassica crops. The flies lay their eggs in the soil and white maggots eat the roots, causing the plants to die back. To prevent an attack, spray the soil around the base of the plants with Lindex and, as further precaution, dip the roots before planting into a paste made up of calomel and water. Dusting the plants with Lindex at regular intervals in summer will also prevent trouble from aphides which winter on the plants.

DOWNY MILDEW   It attacks all brassicas, especially the Brussels sprout, including the young seedlings and also the sprouts, covering them with a grey mould. It also attacks cabbages and it is possible for the fungus to remain alive on decaying leaves in the soil for years. It may also attack the heads of savoys during the latter weeks of winter. Regular spraying with Bordeaux Mixture will prevent an outbreak.

WIREWORM   This pest may prove troublesome to brassica crops and is often prevalent in newly dug soil. It is the grub of the click beetle, being thin and wiry and orange in colour. It will sever and devour the roots of many plants. Treat the soil before planting with Aldrin dust or Gammexane at a strength of 1 oz. per sq. yd. or with napthalene at double the strength. These preparations will also exterminate leather-jackets and millepedes.

VARIETIES

'AVON CROSS' An F1 hybrid which begins to form its sprouts early in autumn, producing even sized sprouts of firm, smooth texture. Unpicked sprouts hold their quality without deterioration.

'PEER GYNT' An F1 hybrid, it is outstanding in every way for it is a plant of compact habit for the small garden, whilst the medium sized sprouts of emerald green are packed so tightly on the stems that it is impossible to place a finger tip between them.

Cabbage *Brassica oleracea*

This is one of the indispensable vegetables for all gardens, with its extreme hardiness and ease of culture. By planting varieties to mature at various times, it is possible to have cabbages for cutting all the year. There are varieties (a) for spring and early summer, (b) for autumn and (c) for winter use.

For spring and summer These will be ready to cut during the sparse late spring and early summer months when the Brussels sprouts have finished and when there are few other vegetables available. The plants never attain the large size of the winter varieties and maturing quickly, remain sweet and tender, never becoming coarse or strongly flavoured.

With spring cabbage, timing is all important for the plants have to be large and strong enough to withstand severe winter weather and yet must not have been grown 'soft' otherwise they are liable to be damaged by hard frost. Again, if too advanced before winter, the plants may 'bolt' before they are ready to use if the early spring weather is dry and warm.

General cultivation A sowing is made in July. Sow thinly in shallow drills made 9 in. apart or broadcast in a prepared seed bed. Keep the soil moist to hasten germination and move the plants to their permanent quarters early in September. The ground should have been well manured for a previous crop. If not, dig in some well decayed manure (old mushroom bed compost is ideal for this crop) and give a 2 oz. per sq. yd. dressing with basic slag at planting time.

Plant 16 in. apart, for spring cabbages retain their compact habit and never grow large. Except for keeping the hoe moving between the plants, they will require no attention other than to give a $\frac{1}{2}$ oz. per sq. yd. dressing of nitrate of soda between the rows, preferably on a rainy day, as soon as growth commences early in spring.

To have spring cabbage at its best, cut off the heads before they become too large. If the stems are left in the ground, a succession of small heads will form where the cabbage head was cut away. These may be used early in summer.

VARIETIES

For spring

'DURHAM ELF'   It is of very compact habit and makes a small pointed heart, dark green in colour and sweet and succulent when cooked.

'GREYHOUND'   Very early to mature, it makes a large pointed heart with few outer leaves and possesses good flavour.

For autumn

To continue the supply when the spring cabbages finish early in June, a number of quick maturing varieties should be ready to cut.

Seed is sown in a frame in September or early in March, the plants being moved to the open ground in April. By August, they will have formed well-hearted heads for cutting until the winter varieties are ready towards the end of the year.

'PRIMO'   Extremely early, it makes a small ball-shaped head which is ready to cut 5 months from sowing.

'TOZANDA'   An F1 hybrid which at the 1970 Scottish Horticultural Research Institute trials, out-yielded all other autumn varieties and gained first place for uniformity. It is ready early October when it will have formed a solid, flat head of blue-green with an ice-white centre when cut. The average weight is about 3 lb.

Japanese flowering cabbages. These colourful ornamental cabbages put an end to the idea that vegetables are unsightly. They can be chopped and used in salads

A well-grown cabbage should have a large, firm heart, and relatively little loose leaf around the edges

For winter

For cutting during winter, sow the late maturing cabbages in April and plant out when large enough to handle. Allow 20–24 in. between the plants for they make larger heads and occupy the ground longer. For this reason, the soil must be well nourished whilst town garden soils should be given a 4 oz. per sq. yd. dressing of nitro-chalk before planting.

Owing to the frequency of club root amongst cabbages and all brassicas, dipping the roots in calomel solution before planting will give control but, as an extra precaution, the plants should be given fresh ground every year on a 4-year rotation.

VARIETIES

'FILLGAP' This matures between the autumn and winter varieties, making a small globular solid head with smooth outer leaves. It will hold its head for many weeks if not cut as soon as ready.

'SENTINEL' This is one of the largest of all cabbages, an average head weighing more than 6 lb. It is a handsome variety with a mild flavour, blue-green in colour with waved outer leaves.

PESTS AND DISEASES

As for Brussels sprouts and broccoli.

Cabbage, Red *Brassica oleracea*

This is a most valuable vegetable for pickling but of all cabbages it is the most difficult to grow well. It requires a long growing season, seed being sown in shallow drills early in September, the plants remaining in the rows during winter.

In spring, the plants are set out 2 ft. apart into a rich soil which has been previously well limed. Just before planting, work into the top-soil a 2 oz. per sq. yd. dressing of super-phosphate and sulphate of potash and plant firmly. A sprinkling of sulphate of ammonia around the roots towards the end of spring will enable the plants to get away to a good start. 'Early Blood Red' will have formed a large head of deepest crimson by the autumn and is delicious cut into shreds and used raw in a winter salad.

Carrot *Daucus carota*

Though a native of the British Isles, it was not until the arrival of the Huguenot refugees who taught us how it should be grown and cooked, that the carrot became an important part of our diet. The most delicious carrots are those grown over a gentle hot bed early in spring, the seed being sown in February, in a frame. If a frame is not available, make a sowing over a hot bed made in a sheltered sunny corner about mid-March when the roots will be ready to use at the end of May.

Sowing Seed is sown broadcast into a finely screened soil. The bed should be kept comfortably moist and whilst the frame must be kept closed when the weather is cold, admit plenty of fresh air on mild days. The young carrots will be ready to pull early in May, the smaller roots being left to mature later in the month. One of the shorter rooted varieties should be grown for forcing such as 'Sweetheart' or 'Early Gem'.

For the maincrop, the ground should be friable and well drained and, as for all roots, should have been manured for a previous crop. Bring the soil to a fine tilth and sow early in April, in shallow drills made 10 in. apart. On land which tends to be heavy, sow the short-rooting varieties.

General cultivation As soon as large enough, the seedlings must be thinned to 2 in. apart in the rows, later removing alternate plants to allow the roots 4 in. in which to mature. Another sowing is made early in June to provide a winter crop.

During dry weather, keep the plants growing by regular waterings and give them an occasional application of dilute liquid manure. Frequent dustings of weathered soot on either side of the rows will encourage early maturity and assist in the control of pests.

As the plants reach maturity, make certain that the tops are not out of the ground and exposed to sunlight, for this will cause them to turn green. They should be lightly earthed up to prevent this condition or given a mulch of strawy manure.

Carrots are not improved by frost and any still in the ground should be lifted before the end of November and stored in boxes of sand in a shed or cellar.

PESTS AND DISEASES

CARROT FLY   The most troublesome of carrot foes, the flies laying their eggs in the soil when the yellow larvae will burrow into the 'carrots' causing considerable damage, and making them virtually useless for any purpose. Dressing the seed before sowing, with Dieldrex 'B' (one-sixteenth of an ounce per 1 oz. of seed) or dusting the soil with Lindex at sowing time and the seedlings when they appear will give complete control.

SPLITTING   A common trouble with carrots. It is a physiological disorder by which the root splits lengthwise. It may be caused by heavy rain following a long period of drought during which time the plants should be watered artificially. A soil deficient in potash may also cause this trouble.

VARIETIES

'CHANTENAY'   Though early to mature, it stores well and is the best for late summer sowing, being a stump rooted carrot of first class flavour and good texture.

'EARLY NANTES'   This forces well, the long, tubular roots being uniform in size and shape whilst the quality and flavour are outstanding.

'GOLDINHART'   This grows 6 in. long and is 2 in. thick at the shoulder, tapering to a stumpy point. Its orange flesh continues through to the centre with almost complete lack of core, making it outstanding for freezing and canning.

Cauliflower   *Brassica oleracea*

For an early summer crop, seed is sown in a cold frame or under cloches early in September, and in October the young plants are pricked out into another part of the frame where they remain until April. The seed bed must not be too rich but it must not lack lime. After sowing, water with Cheshunt Compound, 1 oz. dissolved in 2 gal. of water, to prevent the seedlings being attacked by Black Leg, but water as little as possible during winter.

General cultivation After hardening, set out the plants early in April, spacing them 2 ft. apart. The early varieties will begin to form heads in July and these are followed by plants obtained from a sowing made outdoors in spring.

To make large heads, cauliflowers require a soil rich in humus and plant food. The land must first be well limed, then dig in some strawy manure and material from the compost heap. Hop manure is excellent for cauliflowers whilst northern gardeners will find wool shoddy readily obtainable and a valuable source of nitrogen and humus.

To make close compact heads, the plants also need potash which should be given as sulphate of potash at the rate of 2 oz. per sq. yd. just before planting. At the same time give a similar dressing of superphosphate of lime which will help to promote vigorous root action. Should the spring be cold and the plants slow to start growing, dust around each a sprinkling of nitrate of soda given on a rainy day.

As the heads quickly run to seed, especially during dry weather, it is preferable to grow small numbers of plants for succession rather than to make a large sowing of a particular variety which will mature at the same time. Firm planting will reduce the tendency for the plants to go to seed prematurely.

To protect the curds (heads) from dirt and strong sunshine, fold over one or two of the outer leaves as the heads begin to form and so that they will be clean and white when cut.

PESTS AND DISEASES

BROWNING A condition which attacks the cauliflower rather than the cabbage and is caused by a lack of the trace element, boron. The leaves grow narrow and may turn brown whilst the curd is bitter and unpalatable. In cabbage, the leaves curl at the edges and there is cracking of the stems. It is corrected by manuring with borax at the rate of 1 oz. per 60 sq. yd., merely a trace.

CABBAGE CATERPILLAR The small grubs hatch out from the eggs of the Cabbage White butterfly and penetrate to the

Cauliflower 'Unwins Snocap', an extra early very large-heading variety
Courtesy W. J. Unwin Ltd.

To grow good carrots you need a carefully prepared, stone-free bed. Stones distort the shape of the carrot. Too rich a soil (i.e. one freshly manured) will make them split

centre of the curds. To prevent an attack, dust the plants with derris powder from early June, before the curds begin to form.

VARIETIES

'ALL THE YEAR ROUND' This may be sown any time for frame culture and open ground planting for it will mature throughout the year depending on date of sowing. It forms large milk-white curds protected by large green leaves.

'DWARF MONARCH' Of compact habit and ideal for a small garden, its small white heads are ready to use early September from a late spring sowing.

'EARLY SNOWBALL' Of dwarf, compact habit it may be grown in a frame to mature early in spring; or from an early sowing it will mature early in summer, its close firm heads being of medium size.

'VEITCH'S SELF-PROTECTING' The hardiest of all, its large incurved leaves affording protection to its milk-white curds until January when the broccolis are ready to cut.

Celery *Apium graveolens*

Two sowings should be made, one of the self-blanching to use from the latter weeks of summer until the late autumn; another of the ordinary white or pink variety to use through winter. This will be crisp and tender only after hard frost. It requires more labour in its culture than the self-blanching type.

(i) Self-blanching The culture of this type of celery has greater appeal to the amateur as it does not require trenching. It is grown on the flat in a soil which has been deeply worked and well manured, decayed strawy manure being most suitable, whilst any other materials which will enable the soil to retain moisture should be provided.

The plants are set out early in June about 9 in. apart. Plant firmly and never allow them to lack moisture or they will grow tough and stringy. Early in September the first roots will be ready to lift and should be used as soon as possible. Eaten raw or braised, this celery has a mild, nutty flavour and, if grown well, the sticks will be crisp and tender.

VARIETY

GOLDEN SELF-BLANCHING   This is the best to grow, the heart being of purest white and self-folding. However, it should be said that where the sticks are required for eating raw, they will be more succulent if pieces of cardboard are fastened round the stems about 3 weeks before they are to be used. The lengths of cardboard should be cut beforehand to the requisite size and be tied in place with raffia near the top and bottom of the stalks. Earthing up is not necessary for with close planting and being self-folding, they will blanch themselves but will be made more tender if light is excluded for several weeks before lifting.

(ii) Non self-blanching   This is the more familiar celery, mostly cultivated by market gardeners to supply the wholesale markets during winter.

Most celery is grown in the black fenland soil of East Anglia, elsewhere it requires a heavy loam retentive of summer moisture. It also needs to be grown in trenches which should be enriched with decayed manure, augmented by garden compost or peat. As the trench is prepared, the humus materials should be well trodden down, for firm planting is essential. Make the trench 12 in. deep and if it is made sufficiently wide, a double row is planted so as to obtain the most economic use of the compost.

Sowing   To be successful, celery must be grown well from the beginning and raising the plants demands care. Should the seedlings be left too long before transplanting, they will become 'hard' and may run to seed if the summer is dry. Taking 4 weeks to germinate, the seed must be sown early enough to have made good-sized plants to set out early in June. This means sowing in a frame over a gentle hot bed or warmed by soil heating cables about mid-March.

The traditional method of growing celery is in trenches. Blanching is achieved by gradually filling in the trench. The heaps of soil on either side of the trench can be used for growing early potatoes, the soil being returned to the trench when the potatoes are lifted

Sow thinly and as soon as the seed has germinated; admit fresh air whenever the days are mild. The seedlings are transplanted to frames or are set out in rows beneath cloches, setting them 2 in. apart and here they remain until ready for the open ground about June 1st. They should not be planted out until they have been gradually hardened off.

Plant out on a dull, showery day and moisten the roots before doing so. If the trench is filled in to within 3 in. of the top, this will enable the plants to receive moisture from the surrounding soil and will make it easier for earthing up. Plant 10 in. apart in a double row, but allowing 12 in. for the most vigorous varieties such as 'Lancashire Prize Red'. Keep the plants damp by frequent waterings whilst an occasional watering with dilute liquid manure from early July will help to build up plants of top quality.

Blanching This calls for care. In late July, when the plants are about 12 in. high, they should be earthed up at the base as for potatoes, but full blanching should not be done until the plants have stopped growing. A second earthing up is done at the end of August and again a month later whilst the soil is still friable. At this time, the plants are tied at the top with strong twine or with raffia to prevent the soil reaching the heart. This may be done by using a long length of twine and looping it around the top of each plant in the row without cutting the twine. More soil may then be earthed up, and by early November the plants will be comfortably blanched.

Celery is not lifted before the first sharp frost which is considered necessary to improve its quality, ensuring that crispness which is the hallmark of good celery. Take care when lifting, that the soil does not reach the heart, which will prove difficult to clean if it does. Begin lifting at the end of the row, first pulling back the soil and pressing the fork well into the ground so that the plant may be lifted without damage to the stems. Then trim off the roots and wash free of soil.

PESTS AND DISEASES

CELERY FLY It lays its eggs on the foliage during the midsummer months, the larvae attacking the leaves causing them to blister and decay. The blisters may be pinched to kill the maggots but to prevent an attack, spray the foliage during June and July with quassi solution which will prevent the flies from laying their eggs. As the flies will lay several times, it is necessary to repeat the spraying at intervals of 3 weeks.

LEAF SPOT   This attacks the foliage, especially in damp, humid weather, first as small brown spots on the leaves. These rapidly increase in size and under magnification will be seen to be covered with black dots which are the fruiting bodies. Soon the foliage will turn brown and die. Spraying with Bordeaux Mixture shortly after the plants are set out and again before earthing up will prevent an outbreak. It is also advisable to sow seed which has been treated for Leaf Spot as recommended by the Ministry of Agriculture.

VARIETIES

'CLUSEED DWARF WHITE'   An interesting celery for a small garden for it grows only half the height of ordinary varieties and makes a large, solid heart. It is late to mature and improves with the frosts.

'LANCASHIRE PRIZE RED'   This makes a large, solid plant, ideal for exhibition, the sticks being pale red and with outstanding flavour.

Cucumber *Cucumis sativus*

Where cold frames or barn-type cloches are available, the frame cucumbers may be grown; where there is no glass then one may still enjoy summer cucumbers by growing those known as ridge cucumbers. These are the hardiest of all the forms, those for frames being also suitable for growing in a heated greenhouse. For flavour and tenderness the frame varieties are the equal of green-house cucumbers and as they are most prolific and easily grown they should be more widely cultivated. Even more delicious is the apple cucumber, which is so mild and tender that those who suffer after-effects from other varieties will suffer none from this unique variety.

With all types of the cucumber they are usually allowed to grow too large before removing them. This not only greatly reduces the quality but also the cropping capacity of the plant.

Frame cucumbers These are prolific, and will be the equal in appearance of greenhouse grown fruits, and have a much better flavour. If they have a disadvantage it is·that being in frames through the summer, the plants will require detailed attention as to watering and ventilation. But the trouble is well worth while for they will continue to fruit until October.

Though frame cucumbers may be grown quite cold in a manured bed, growing over a gentle hot bed will result in an earlier crop and give an additional month's fruiting.

The hot bed is made up at the end of March, the compost being placed 18 in. deep in the frames and covered with 6 in. of soil. When the bed temperature has fallen to just below 80 °F the seed is sown. As cucumbers resent root disturbance, the seed is best sown where the plants are to grow, rather than in small pots as for marrows. Where two 5 ft. × 4 ft. lights are together, the frame will accommodate three plants, two seeds being sown close together in three parts of the frame, the strongest plant in each group being retained.

If no hot bed is being used, then the soil should be enriched to a depth of 6–8 in. with well decayed strawy manure. The seed is sown early in April and, being slower to germinate owing to lack of bottom heat, the plants will bear fruit a month later. If two frames are available, it is better to delay planting the seed until early May so that the plants will be bearing their largest number of fruits when the hot bed plants have passed their peak.

After sowing the seed into soil made damp, cover with the lights and place sacking over them at night to retain as much heat as possible. Keep the frames closed to maintain a warm, damp atmosphere until the seed has germinated. The sacking should be placed over the lights each night until the end of May, for hard frosts are often experienced until that time. Should the temperature of the frame fall due to the hot bed losing its heat, fresh compost is placed round the frame boards to give additional warmth, especially at night.

Keep the plants moist but not wet, and always use slightly warm water for spraying. Until the end of May, damping down

F₁ hybrid cucumber 'Feminex'. This remarkable cucumber has all female flowers and thus does not need laborious hand-pollinating. It produces enormous crops of good size fruits, and is exceptionally disease resistant. *Courtesy Thompson & Morgan (Ipswich) Limited*

should be done before mid-day, so that the moisture will dry off the plants before the cooler temperature of night. But regular spraying must be done to keep down red spider; cucumbers require a humid atmosphere and a high degree of moisture at their roots. If the plants are kept too dry they will never be a success.

General cultivation As the plants grow, they are trained about the frame, spacing out the shoots and pegging them down so that each has room to develop. The laterals should be stopped at the second leaf, the sub-laterals being trained about the frame.

It is important to remove the fruits before they become too large for they will not only lose texture and flavour, but will crowd the frame, at the same time taking too much out of the plants.

The soil should be kept moist which, during a sunny period, may mean watering twice daily, also syringeing the plants to guard against red spider. Ventilation calls for attention as the early summer sunshine gathers strength. Keep as even a temperature in the frames as possible, so that the plants are not wilting in heat by day and then having to endure greatly reduced temperatures at night. So ventilate freely whenever the day is warm. Hand pollination of the flowers is not necessary.

Before the frame becomes too full of plant growth, give a light top dressing around the roots, using finely sifted loam to which has been added a small quantity of decayed manure. This will provide any surface roots with nourishment, and will act as a mulch in keeping the roots cool and moist. Some peat may also be added or used instead of the manure.

Watering with dilute liquid manure when the first fruits begin to form will result in a vigorous plant and in the formation of a large crop. As the fruits have a tendency to decay as they come into contact with the soil and they may also grow slightly mis-shapen, each fruit should be carefully placed on a flat piece of wood until it has matured and been removed. Glass is used for this purpose but tends to hold moisture, and the fruits may decay on the side next to the glass especially if the weather is dull and the fruits are slow to mature.

Growing under cloches Cucumbers do well under barn-type cloches. Ground the width of the glass should be well enriched with decayed manure to a depth of 12 in. This should be done during March, the glass being placed in position for a full week before the seeds are sown at the end of April. They are best planted 4 ft. apart. Planting in this way gives protection from stem rot. At all times the plants from the seedling stage should be kept well watered, a humid atmosphere being created exactly the same as when growing in frames.

The plants should be stopped at the fourth leaf, two laterals only being allowed to develop, which in turn should be stopped at the fifth leaf. A mulch of peat and soil, regular syringeing during hot weather, and placing narrow pieces of wood beneath the fruit to mature, should be done during the life of the crop. If the plants should make too much foliage as the season advances, defoliation must be done by degrees so as not to upset the balance of the plant.

VARIETIES

(Frame)

'CONQUEROR' A splendid cucumber for a cold frame, long and even in shape with a handsome dark green skin. Does better when given hot-bed cultivation.

'EVERY DAY' A valuable variety in that it will set its fruits well even in a dull summer. The fruits have a smooth dark green skin and are of excellent flavour, whilst they are un-surpassed for exhibition.

Ridge cucumber Where there is neither frame nor cloches available, then the ridge cucumber should be grown, for it is hardy and in an average season will grow well. No plant is more prolific; in fact where cultivations have been generous it will be necessary to look over the plants almost daily, so quickly do the fruits form.

Select a sunny, open position but one where the plants may be given some protection from strong winds. On the balcony of a flat they may be grown and will prove attractive with their handsome foliage. All that is required is a box filled with decayed manure and loam, the seed being germinated by covering the box with a sheet of clean glass.

This is also the method by which the seed is germinated out-doors; if no cloche is available construct a miniature frame with bricks, and cover with a sheet of glass. A miniature hot bed may also be made by removing 2 sq. ft. of soil and filling this to a depth of 9 in. with prepared manure. This is covered with 3 in. of soil which is made level with the surrounding soil. Similar hot beds can be made at intervals of 4 ft. keeping them in line to help with cultivations. Bricks are placed round each, two seeds sown 1 in. deep, the weaker of the two plants being removed. Cucumbers resent transplanting and this is a better method than growing in pots. Simply set the seed where the plants are to fruit.

If the garden is exposed, the plants should be grown between ridges which will provide protection from cold winds, but the soil should be light and friable enabling excess moisture to drain away.

The seed must not be sown before early May, for the plants should not be exposed to the elements before June.

When the plants have formed two or three leaves they should be stopped to encourage the formation of the lateral shoots which will carry the crop. No further restriction will be necessary, but to ensure a heavy crop give a mulch around the roots either of decayed lawn mowings, or with well rotted manure and never allow the plants to lack moisture, otherwise fruits will cease to form. During a dry period and where growing in a light soil, copious amounts of water will be required daily.

VARIETIES

'APPLE CUCUMBER' Of all cucumbers this, in the opinion of connoisseurs of good food, is the most delicious. It is listed by few seedsmen, and rarely found growing in any gardens. The fruits are like pale yellow apples, oval in shape and they should be gathered and used when they have reached the size of small apples, for the plants bear abundantly, and over a long period. Whilst the fruits possess the true refreshing cucumber flavour, they are much more juicy and yet the flesh is crisp.

'BURPEE HYBRID' An F1 hybrid from America bearing handsome dark green fruits in great abundance and in all seasons. The skin is smooth and thin, the flesh crisp and white.

'HAMPSHIRE GIANT' A splendid hardy cucumber, the fruits are more than 12 in. long, the skin pale green, the flesh never coarse, even when left too long on the plants.

'SUTTON'S PROLIFIC' Very hardy and of compact habit, making it popular for small gardens. The medium sized fruit possesses excellent flavour.

PESTS AND DISEASES

GUMMOSIS The fungus causes grey spots on the leaves which burst open whilst they may also occur on the fruits when they will exude a gummy liquid. It occurs mostly in dull

77

wet seasons but may be kept under control by dusting the plants regularly with flowers of sulphur.

LEAF BLOTCH   Small pale green spots appear on the upper surfaces of the leaves. They will increase in size and later turn grey and then brown before falling away to leave holes in the leaves. The fruits may also be attacked. Infected leaves should be removed and burnt whilst spraying with liver of sulphur solution should give control.

POWDERY MILDEW   This may attack plants growing under glass where there is insufficient ventilation. It is recognized by the white mildew-like growth on the leaves and shoot tips. There are now resistant varieties but to control, spray with Shirlan to which is added the spreader Agral N.

Endive   *Cichorum endivia*

Though rarely grown, it has been used as a salad crop since earliest times, for either cooked or eaten raw it has a most delicate flavour and, where grown well, a crispness which is unusual with summer salad crops.

Endive grows best where it is to mature for it will run to seed quickly if transplated and also if there is not sufficient humus in the soil to retain summer moisture. If manure is scarce, dig in some hop manure, peat or decayed leaves, or garden compost for it demands a cool, moist soil which does not dry out quickly in hot weather. For this reason, a heavy soil lightened with humus produces better endives than does a light soil.

Sowing   Do not sow the seed before July 1st for the plants mature better in the cooler conditions of early autumn whilst July is often a month of wet weather which enables the plants to start well.

Sow thinly, in shallow drills made 15 in. apart and when large enough, thin out the seedlings to 10 in. If possible, select a position in semi-shade or ground facing north or east for endive prefers cool conditions.

General cultivation   Water whenever the ground is dry and, early in August, give the plants a weekly application of dilute liquid manure which will improve the quality. If a

Kohl-rabi looks like a cross between a turnip and a swede: it is in fact a swollen-stemmed cabbage

second sowing is made late in July and the plants covered with barn cloches about mid-October, it will be possible to enjoy endive until Christmas for the plants will withstand several degrees of frost.

Blanching is the most important part of its culture. Raffia is tied around the top of the plants as soon as they reach maturity. This should be done when the plants are quite dry. The tying must be done carefully, so as not to cut through the leaves. After 3 weeks, the plants will be blanched and crisp at the centre, a mass of curled leaf and in perfect condition. After blanching, the acrid flavour departs and the foliage becomes sweet and tender.

VARIETIES

'BATAVIAN WHITE' The best flavoured of all endives, making a large full heart of heavily curled leaves which are crisp and tender.

'GIANT FRINGED OYSTER' This makes a large head 15 in. across, filled with rich green lacinated leaves which blanch to creamy white at the centre.

Kohl-rabi *Brassica oleracea*

This may be said to resemble a cross between a turnip and a swede, though it is really a swollen-stemmed cabbage. It forms a large turnip-like globe on the stem, several inches above soil

79

level and if used when about 3 in. across has a mild, sweet turnip-like flavour. It grows quickly, the 'globes' being ready to use within 10 weeks of sowing.

Kohl-rabi requires a light, sandy soil, enriched with some decayed manure. Old mushroom bed compost is ideal, whilst anything which will enable the soil to retain moisture should be dug in.

Sowing Make the first sowing early in April, in drills made 15 in. apart and thin out to 9 in. in the rows. Sowings may be made once each month from April until early July so that the early 'globes' can be used when small, whilst those from later sowings may be left to stand over winter.

Do not peel them, merely trim off the roots and remove the leaves; then cook as for turnips or swedes. They should never be allowed to grow too large.

This is a plant which is not troubled by hot, dry conditions and when the turnip is often fibrous and unpleasant, the kohl-rabi retains its delicate flavour. It requires no special care in its culture and is troubled neither by pest nor disease.

So quickly does it mature that an early crop may be obtained by sowing in March over a mild hot bed in a frame when the 'globes' will be ready to cut before the end of May.

VARIETIES

'EARLY PURPLE VIENNA' This takes slightly longer to mature than 'Early White' and stands better over winter. The 'globes' have a purple skin whilst the flesh is greenish-white, being tender and mild of flavour.

'EARLY WHITE VIENNA' Quick to mature, this variety has a smooth pale green skin and a creamy white flesh which is sweet and mild.

Leek *Allium ampeloprasum* var. *porrum*

To grow leeks well, the soil should be trenched and heavy soils lightened by incorporating some peat or garden compost and a quantity of grit or boiler ash. Excessive manuring is not desirable and leeks are best planted in ground which has been manured for a previous crop.

Where trenching, remove the soil to the width of a spade and 10 in. deep and at the bottom place some garden compost. This is covered with friable soil in good 'heart' into which some peat has been incorporated, together with 1 oz. per sq. yd. of superphosphate and $\frac{1}{2}$ oz. of sulphate of potash. An idea is to throw up the soil on both sides of the trench so that the fertilizers may be added to the soil on one side which is replaced, whilst the soil on the other side is used for blanching the leeks as they grow.

Sowing Seed is sown about mid-March in shallow drills and covered with cloches to hasten germination, or sow in frames for the leek requires a long growing season to produce a large succulent 'stick'. Keep the seed moist when it will soon germinate and the plants will be ready to set out before the end of June. This is essential if large 'sticks' are to be obtained.

When planting, make a hole 6 in. deep with a dibber, into which the plants are dropped. Do not fill in the hole with soil but when planting is complete, water in. A double row should be made in the trench, planting 9 in. apart and staggering the plants with the rows about 6 in. from each other. When planting, allow the side part of the leaf, the blade, to fall along the row rather than across it.

Leeks are lovers of moisture and must be kept well provided with it. If not, the leeks will remain small and will be tough and woody after cooking.

Blanching Early in August, corrugated paper held in place with a rubber band is placed around the lower part of the plant. This will help to 'draw' it and at the same time will blanch the stem. From then onwards as the plants make growth, the soil thrown up on one side of the trench is placed around the plants to complete the blanching. Earthing up must be done with care so that the soil does not enter the folds of the leaves.

Feeding with a weak solution of dried blood or liquid manure during autumn will help to build up large, succulent 'sticks'.

An additional help to forming a large 'stick' is to clip back the leaves to half their length, at regular intervals from the time the plants are set out. If not done, the plants will form excess leaf at the expense of stem which is the edible part. The plants will continue to grow until mid-November when the first liftings are made with a fork and the soil washed away.

Leeks need a good, rich stone-free soil and plenty of moisture throughout the growing season if large, succulent 'sticks' are to be produced

Further liftings will take place during winter when required, for no matter how severe the weather the plants will suffer no harm.

PESTS AND DISEASES

EELWORM   Many bulbous plants are attacked by this pest, a nematode which lays its eggs in the bulbous root, the young, upon hatching, feeding on the living cells and causing the leaves to turn yellow. If an attack has been noticed on plants previously occupying the same ground, treat the soil with Jeyes Fluid (2 tablespoons to a gallon of water) several weeks before the leeks are planted.

WHITE TIP   A fungus which attacks the leaf tips, causing them to turn yellow, then white with the leaf finally entering a state of decay when the plants will fall over at soil level. If caught in time, the disease will be arrested by spraying the plants with weak Burgundy Mixture or with a copper fungicide applied as a dust.

VARIETIES

'CLANDON WHITE' An early leek, producing large 'sticks' in autumn from a February sowing. The foliage is dark green, the stems of great length and of sweet, mild flavour.

'MARBLE PILLAR' This produces the longest blanched stem of any variety and is ideal for exhibition, being pure white when blanched and of mild, sweet flavour.

'YATE'S EMPIRE' A late variety which will stand until April, the leaf blades broad and dark green, the stems long, thick and sturdy, snow-white when blanched.

Lettuce *Lactuca sativa*

It is the backbone of salads throughout the year, and a continuous supply of crisp, home-grown lettuce is one of the gardener's delights.

More than almost any other crop it requires a well nourished soil enriched with plenty of decayed manure. Old mushroom bed compost is especially suitable or used hops obtainable from a brewery and as much humus as can be obtained should be dug into the soil which must be retentive of summer moisture.

Equally important is a well limed soil for one of an acid nature, however slight will, in damp weather, cause the plants to grow limp and slimy. If peat is used, and it is an excellent provider of humus, give additional lime.

Those who possess a cold frame or cloches will be able to have an all the year round supply, the seed being sown at intervals. By using a small part of a frame in which the seed is sown broadcast, or by sowing in shallow drills under cloches in autumn, a spring and early summer crop may be enjoyed. By sowing in the open from spring until early autumn, lettuce may be cut from mid-summer until Christmas whilst in the more favourable parts, unprotected sowings can be made in the open to provide an all the year round supply.

Sowing Seed is sown in a seed bed and the young plants are moved to where they are to mature, as soon as large enough to handle. If a sowing is made outdoors in March, the plants will have hearted by the beginning of June when the usually warm weather brings with it a greater demand for salads.

The secret of growing good lettuce is to keep the plants on the move by giving them a well prepared soil, yet they must always be grown 'hard' otherwise they will fall a victim to mildew. Artificial fertilizers should not be used, apart from sulphate of potash which will encourage the plants to grow 'hard'. At planting time, 2 oz. per sq. yd. should be raked into the soil.

Transplanting should be done in showery weather for the plants may not recover if moved when the ground is dry. The seedlings should be moved early, before they form a tap root but if transplanting is delayed, cut off the tap root before replanting. The plants will then heart more quickly.

Plant on the flat, spacing out to the requirements of each variety for some grow dwarf and compact, whilst others such as 'Webb's Wonderful', make hearts 18 in. across. They may be set out between rows of dwarf peas or beans, or inter-cropped with late maturing 'greens' such as cauliflower or cabbage.

The modern cos lettuce is self-blanching or self-folding and there is no need to tie the heads with raffia as of old in order to induce them to form a solid heart.

Growing under glass For a winter crop, sow the seed early in September and transplant to a frame in October. If the frame soil is heated by cables or if the plants are to be grown over a hot bed, they will quickly heart up and will have made sizeable plants for cutting by the year end. The soil should be friable but not too rich in nitrogenous manure otherwise the plants will be liable to suffer from mildew. Keep the soil on the dry side, giving only sufficient moisture to maintain plant growth. Plant 8 in. apart and to guard against mildew, dust the plants with flowers of sulphur once each fortnight until they begin to heart.

If the frame is heated, ventilate on all suitable days but where the plants are grown cold, the minimum of ventilation (and moisture) should be permitted. During periods of hard frost, cover the lights at night with canvas or sacking which is removed during the day unless the weather is especially severe. Where growing in a Dutch-light house, the plants will require similar culture and where grown cold, they will not be ready to cut until March.

A frame may be used to protect the plants during winter. They should then be moved to the open ground in March after hardening. From a sowing made early in October, plant the seedlings 2 in. apart in the frame, ventilate on all suitable occasions and keep the plants dry. If planted out towards the end of March, the frame may be used for tomatoes or marrows whilst the lettuce will be ready to cut early in May.

PESTS AND DISEASES

BOTRYTIS   This appears on the leaves as a grey mould causing them to decay and is most prevalent amongst plants growing under glass and during damp, humid summers. Dusting young plants with Orthocide Captan dust will normally prevent an outbreak.

DOWNY MILDEW   This mostly attacks plants growing in frames or under cloches, appearing as a white powder on the underside of the leaves. There are a number of resistant lettuce varieties, but an outbreak may be prevented by dusting plants growing under glass with a mixture of equal parts lime and sulphur.

MILLEPEDE   This is the most troublesome of lettuce pests, attacking the roots of young plants, causing them to wilt. The pest is almost black in colour and moves slowly. When touched, it rolls itself up into a ball. It may be exterminated by treating the soil with Aldrin dust or Gammexane at the rate of 1 oz. per sq. yd. when the beds are prepared.

ROOT APHIS   This attacks the roots of plants both under glass and outdoors, causing the leaves to turn yellow and the plants to wilt. It may be prevented or exterminated by watering the soil before planting or later, if proving troublesome, with Lindex solution.

Lettuce 'Salad Bowl', one of the newer varieties. It is small growing and strongly flavoured. The leaves remain crisp even in the hottest weather

VARIETIES

For winter and early spring (outdoors)

'ARCTIC KING'   For autumn sowing, a cabbage lettuce forming a large solid head with few outer leaves.

'WINTER DENSITY'   The best cos for autumn sowing, making a large dark green head with a good heart.

'WINTER MARVEL'   Sow in autumn and in spring the large cabbage-like heads will be filled with wavy waxy-like leaves which make delicious eating.

For winter and early spring (under glass)

'SUZAN'   One of the best for frame culture, this variety matures early and makes a large dense heart with crisp outer leaves of emerald green.

'TOM THUMB'   An excellent lettuce for a cold frame or cloche culture: may be sown all the year round. The hearts are of cricket ball size, sweet and succulent.

86

Cabbage lettuce 'Suzan'. Lettuces can be ready for the table over a very long season if sown in succession. *Courtesy W. J. Unwin Ltd.*

Cos lettuce 'Giant Perfection', one of the finest cos lettuces ever raised, firm hearted and slow to bolt. *Courtesy W. J. Unwin Ltd.*

For spring and summer sowing (outdoors)

'BUTTERCRUNCH'   A cos though with something of the cabbage varieties, the leaves being olive green, the heart crisp and succulent and never becomes bitter.

'HISTON CRISPIE'   A cos lettuce of excellent qualities and attractive appearance, with pale green crinkled leaves, firmly folding into a large heart of delicious flavour.

'SUGAR COS'   May be said to be a cross between a cabbage and a cos and is outstanding in every way, forming an erect head of medium size which hearts well and which, for its rich sweet flavour, has no equal.

'WEBB'S WONDERFUL'   The finest summer lettuce being highly resistant to disease, the hearts remaining crisp and succulent through the hottest weather whilst it does not easily run to seed.

87

Marrows, Pumpkins and Squashes
Cucurbita spp

These terms are interchangeable, for the marrows, pumpkins and summer squashes are all varieties of *Cucurbita pepo*. The winter squashes, however, are varieties of *Cucurbita maxima*.

Marrows should be planted in full sun and where they may be sheltered from cold winds. They resent root disturbance, so must be grown in pots. One method is to raise the plants over a hot bed made in a frame and sowing the seed at the end of March. Over the compost is placed 3 in. of fine soil and into this is pressed $2\frac{1}{2}$-in. pots touching each other. The pots are filled with John Innes sowing compost, in which peat is substituted by well decayed manure, old mushroom bed compost being ideal.

The seeds are pressed into the compost, their pointed end towards the top and just covered with the compost. The pots are given a thorough soaking and the frames are kept closed until germination has taken place, watering whenever necessary. During the first 3 weeks of April the frames should be covered with sacking at night if frost is expected.

Early in May, when the plants have formed their second pair of leaves, they will be ready for removal to a cold frame for hardening. This is done by first leaving off the glass during the daytime, then gradually at night, so that by the month end the plants will be ready to go out.

Soil preparation When manure was plentiful, one would plant marrows on heaps of compost, and how well they grew. Today these heaps have been reduced to minute hillocks and the plants make little headway, especially in a warm, dry summer which should suit them well. The reason is not that they lack nourishment but moisture, these little mounds drying out too readily which is fatal to the marrow, for it requires plenty of moisture about its roots.

With the shortage of compost, it is better to plant on the flat, into a soil containing plenty of humus – some decayed manure, peat, spent hops, even decayed leaves or bark fibre being incorporated. If the soil is heavy or the ground low lying then make a raised bed, but work in the same quantity of humus.

Set out the plants at the end of May allowing 3–4 ft. for the bush varieties, and 5–6 ft. for the trailers. Where growing under barn cloches (and this is an excellent crop to grow under glass) make the beds to fit the cloches and plant out early in May. The glass may be removed mid-June, when the plants will have made considerable growth.

If no frame is available, the plants may be grown entirely under cloches and, though the crop will not be so early to mature, it will prove earlier than where the seed is sown in the open. Plants sown over a hot bed will be showing fruit before seedlings raised in the open have made their second leaves.

Those able to obtain manure could raise an early crop by making up a hot bed in the open early in April, covering with 6 in. of soil and sowing the seed under a barn cloche, covering the ends with glass to retain the warmth.

Plant firmly and press the small pot into the soil about 2 in. from the plant, water being given through the pot when required. Before knocking the plant from the pot, water it to bind the roots so that there is no root disturbance.

When the plants have made about 18 in. of growth, pinch out the leader shoots to encourage the formation of side shoots, and to ensure a heavy crop which will set well. Under glass, give daily syringeing to flowers and foliage whenever the weather is warm, and those growing in the open should be kept free from weeds and heavily watered during dry weather. A mulch of peat and decayed strawy manure will be appreciated, so will regular watering with liquid manure from the time the first fruits form. This will be about July 1st from early sown seed in the south; 3–4 weeks later in the north.

The fruits are removed when they have attained a reasonable size: to allow them to remain on the plants until they have become too large will not only reduce the quality but will also reduce the crop. Removing the fruits quickly will enable others to form.

Care must be taken in removing the fruits or the plants may be damaged. Cut away the marrow where it lies rather than lifting it first, for this will disturb the plant. At the same time carefully remove any dead foliage. Handle the fruits carefully so as not to cause bruising.

Pollinating This may be done by insects, especially during dry, sunny periods. However, the plants will begin to fruit earlier and bear heavier crops with artificial pollination.

This may take place in two ways, either by dusting the male flowers and transferring the pollen to those of the female, or by removing the male flower, folding back its petals and pressing it into the female flower. This is done only on a dry day, when the pollen is dry, and when the flowers are open and the pollen ripe. Plants growing under glass will benefit most by this artificial pollination.

No difficulty should be experienced in telling which flower is the male and which the female, for the latter has a tiny marrow-like swelling of the stem immediately beneath the flower. The male is without this swelling.

PESTS AND DISEASES

MILDEW   This also attacks cucumbers growing outdoors and appears as a white powdery mildew on the underside of the leaves. If unchecked, the foliage will turn brown and fall off. Routine spraying with weak Bordeaux Mixture will prevent an outbreak; or spray with liver of sulphur (1 oz. to 3 gal. of water).

VARIETIES

'AVOCADELLA'   A summer marrow of bush habit bearing at the centre of the plant small fruits about the size of a large orange but deep green in colour. The fruit ripens early September. It is also known as the Argentine Marrow, and is popular in that country served cold, as it should be. A delicious way of serving is to boil it for half an hour, then allow it to become quite cold, cutting the marrow in two, removing the pulp and placing in a refrigerator for an hour. Remove half an hour before using and fill the centre with whipped cream. The flesh is pale pink.

'BUTTERNUT'   Of trailing habit this is one of the most delicious of marrows. It keeps well into winter, the fine-textured flesh being at its best when baked. The fruits attain a length of 12 in. and are as thick as one's forearm.

'COCOZELLE' The Italian marrow. This is a semi-trailing variety, to be eaten during August. Removed from the plant when 9 in. long, it is delicious filled with peeled tomatoes, after cooking and cooling and served cold with salad oil or mayonnaise. Dark green with yellow stripes, the marrows will reach 2 ft. in length but will be past their best for eating if allowed to grow so large.

'GOLD NUGGET' An American introduction, each plant bears 6–8 marrows of deep golden yellow striped with white and of the size of a large orange. They make for delicious eating and store well. It is a bush marrow of compact habit.

'ROTHERSIDE ORANGE' A richly flavoured little marrow, bearing fruits the size of a large grapefruit and of the same colour. It is a trailer for summer use and is almost like a melon. It should be cooked, then cooled in a refrigerator and served with sugar or ginger. Add cream or oil to suit one's taste.

'SUTTON'S SUPERLATIVE' A bush marrow, tender and delicious. The fruits are of bottle-green colour, the flesh deep orange and sweet. Though it will grow to exhibition size, the fruits should be used when small.

'TABLE DAINTY' One of the earliest marrows to fruit, it is most prolific. The fruits are small, deep green, striped with a paler green. It is a summer marrow of trailing habit and may be used either hot or cold.

'ZUCCHINI' An F1 hybrid bearing dark green cylindrical fruits like the old 'Long Green Trailing' but of bushy habit. The marrows are best used when 6–8 in. long when they will be tender and of excellent flavour. It does not keep.

Mustard and Cress *Sinapis alba* and *Lepidium sativum*

This crop presents few difficulties and may be grown all the year to use in salads and in sandwiches with cream cheese. Mustard is properly *Sinapis alba*, though commercial growers often substitute Rape, *Brassica napus*, which is quicker to mature: Cress is *Lepidium sativum*.

Sowings should be made every 2–3 weeks throughout the year, during the colder months under glass, and outdoors during warmer weather, in small beds of finely sifted soil. Small boxes may be sown with seed in winter and placed in the kitchen window, to provide fresh 'green' for salads and for garnishing when it is usually scarce. In a temperature of 48 °F the cress will be ready to cut within 2–3 weeks. If mustard, with its sharper flavour is also required, sow the cress four days earlier so that both will be ready to cut together. This is done by taking sufficient in one hand as required to fill a punnet (in which it is marketed) and cutting just above the soil in a single sweep with a sharp knife.

VARIETY

'MOSS CURLED' The best form of cress for it makes plenty of 'head' and is curled and branching, like parsley. It is dark green with a mild but distinct flavour.

Onion *Allium cepa*

To obtain large globular bulbs, it is necessary to give the onion a long season of growth and in the colder parts of Britain this is possible only if sets are planted rather than seed. North of a line drawn from Chester to the Wash, it will be necessary to raise seedlings under glass, preferably in a warm greenhouse, otherwise in an average summer they will fail to attain maximum size and to complete their ripening.

Preparing the soil As onions may be grown in the same ground year after year, a special bed may be prepared, incorporating humus to a depth of 2 ft. together with some well decayed manure. At the same time, work in 4 oz. per sq. yd. of basic slag and 2 oz. of sulphate of potash just before the sets are planted; or give a liberal dressing of bonfire ash. The bed should be brought to a fine tilth and be allowed time to settle before planting. Some growers famed for their mammoth onions will roll the bed before planting.

The sets are pressed into the soil, allowing 6 in. between the bulbs and 12 in. between the rows. The best variety to grow from sets is 'Stuttgarter Riesen'. The sets should be firm and plump and 15–20 mm. in circumference. This variety makes a large bulb which keeps well through winter, and does not 'bolt' in warm weather.

Growing from seed   Where growing from seed (and 1 oz. of seed will produce sufficient plants for a 100 ft. row spacing the plants 6–7 in. apart) sow in a cold frame or in boxes in a heated greenhouse containing John Innes compost. Sow mid-January when the seedlings will be ready to transplant into deep boxes containing a slightly richer compost, early in March. If raising the plants in heat, provide a temperature of 50 °F and harden the plants before they go out.

Seed may also be sown under cloches early in February or, in the warmest parts, in October and may stand unprotected over winter. An additional advantage with autumn sown onions is that they rarely suffer from onion fly attacks. Sow thinly in shallow drills and dust with calomel before sowing.

The plants should go out into prepared beds early in April. Lift them from the boxes as they are required so as not to expose the roots to the sun or a drying wind unduly and plant so that the bulbous part is half out of the ground. Before planting, dip the roots into calomel paste as protection against onion fly and as a further precaution, dust with calomel four weeks later.

Whilst growing, keep the hoe moving between the rows and water copiously in dry weather. A weekly feed with dilute manure water will increase the size of the bulbs. By mid-August, watering should be withheld to enable the bulbs to finish ripening and in this they will be assisted if the tops are bent over, just above the necks, to prevent them from seeding.

Harvesting   At the end of September, when the soil is dry, the bulbs are lifted and laid out on the soil to complete their drying. They are then cleaned of any loose skin and the tops removed, leaving only a small portion necessary to string them together and hang them in a dry, airy shed to be used when required. If the autumn is dry after a wet summer, the bulbs should be left as long as possible before lifting and should then be left on a stone path for fully a week to dry completely. If excess moisture remains in the bulbs, they will begin to grow again in storage and may decay.

Onions need a long growing season if large, round globes are to be produced. The top-growth has not fallen over: it is bent over to encourage ripening of the globes

PESTS AND DISEASES

DOWNY MILDEW   This attacks the plants late in their life, a white coating of fungus appearing on the leaves which, if unchecked, die back leaving the bulbs unable to develop. It is most prevalent in a wet season but may be controlled by dusting the plants with a mixture of lime and sulphur or by spraying with sulphide of potassium, 1 oz. dissolved in 2 gal. of water.

ONION FLY   By far the most troublesome pest: the flies lay their eggs in the soil during May and June, then the maggots tunnel into the bulbs causing the leaves to turn yellow and making the bulbs useless for any purpose. Dusting the rows with calomel before sowing and dipping the roots of young plants into calomel solution before planting will prevent an attack.

94

SMUT   This attacks seedlings at soil level and is so destructive that the Ministry of Agriculture has classified it as a 'notifiable' disease. Black spots appear on the bulb scales and leaves and cause the plants to die back: the spores can remain active in the soil for 20 years or more. Immersing the seed in formalin (1 pt. to 16 gal. of water) for an hour before planting will ensure freedom. Formalin is a poison and must be used with care.

VARIETIES

'AILSA CRAIG'   The best all-purpose onion for it makes a large bulb of deep golden-yellow and is ideal for exhibition. It is an excellent keeper.

'RELIANCE'   A flat onion of great keeping qualities, it makes a large firm bulb of mildest flavour and does well in all soils. It gives best results from an autumn sowing.

Onions, Spring

No summer salad is complete without its spring onions which are raised from seed sown in shallow drills in October and again in early spring. Those from an autumn sowing will be ready to pull early in April, those from a spring sowing being ready from June onwards.

It is important to keep the ground free from weeds so allow 10 in. between the rows to allow for hoeing. Dust the rows with calomel before sowing and when the seedlings appear, give a dressing of weathered soot between the rows to absorb the winter sunlight and warm the soil. Early in the year, give a light sprinkling between the rows of nitrate of soda, preferably during wet weather. This will encourage the plants to make some size.

As they begin to swell at the base, lift and use the largest plants first.

VARIETIES

'WHITE LISBON'   Most commonly used for pulling 'green' in spring owing to its hardiness and mild flavour.

'WHITE SPANISH' A bunching onion of mild and distinctive flavour. It is also suitable for autumn sowing.

Parsnip *Pastinaca sativa*

A British native, it has been appreciated by epicures since earliest times. It is somewhat neglected by modern gardeners for it requires a long season to mature and a deeply worked soil when it is capable of producing a root 3 ft. in length or even longer.

It should be given a soil not lacking in lime and one which has been manured for a previous crop, though humus materials may be dug into a depth of 2–3 ft. The parsnip requires a light friable soil and, where strawy manure or old mushroom bed compost has been used for a previous crop, so much the better. All large stones should be removed before sowing as it is necessary for the long roots to descend straight down into the ground.

To grow for kitchen use, sow in drills 18 in. apart and thin the seedlings first to 5 in. then to 10 in. apart in the rows. It should be said that only fresh seed should be sown. Even if two years old, parsnip seed will fail to germinate. If any seed is left over from a sowing, it should be thrown away. Even fresh seed will germinate irregularly and it should not be sown too thinly.

The best parsnips are grown by the bore-hole system. After preparing the soil to a depth of 2 ft. and allowing the seed bed to consolidate, holes are made at intervals of 12 in. in rows 18 in. apart. Each hole is made about 1 in. in diameter and 18 in. deep and is filled up with a mixture of finely sifted soil, peat, wood ash and anything which will make the compost friable. This is lightly pressed into the hole with a wooden dibber until it reaches the bottom and the hole is gradually filled in and marked by a stake. Two seeds are sown in March at the top of each, just covering them with soil. The weakest seedling is removed when sufficiently large.

Feeding with liquid manure once a fortnight from the end of June will help to form those large succulent roots which are the envy of all who see them on the show bench.

The roots will be ready to lift early November and care is needed so that the tapering roots are not damaged. They may be stored in boxes of sand or left in the ground until required. Like turnips, parsnips are improved with frosting.

PESTS AND DISEASES

CANKER   It is the only serious disease to trouble the parsnip. An outbreak may occur if growing in freshly manured soil or in a soil lacking in lime. It begins at the crown, a small part of which turns brown, then large cracks form around the root which takes on a scabby appearance. There is no known cure but an outbreak may be prevented by correct cultivation whilst there are a number of resistant varieties.

VARIETIES

'AVONRESISTER'   This has a high resistance to canker and should be grown in preference to others where this disease has been experienced. The roots are small but uniform in size so that they need be thinned to only 4 in. apart.

'HOLLOW CROWN'   This variety is hollow at the crown and is one of the most handsome varieties, the roots being long and tapering and of excellent size with a clear bright skin.

Peas   *Pisum sativum*

Today, the pea has an all-year popularity and when not in season, the canned and frozen product is in great demand.

By planting early, mid-season and late maturing varieties, it is possible to have a succession of crops from the end of May until early autumn. Those gardening in the south may take the first sowing in autumn and there will usually be no need to protect the plants as there is in northern gardens where this is usually done by covering them with barn-type cloches. These are placed over the plants early in December but should be removed whenever the weather is mild. The round-seeded varieties should be used for winter planting for they do not hold moisture as do the wrinkle-seeded varieties, the first of which were raised early in the 19th century by Andrew Knight.

The marrow fat peas are wrinkled because some of the starch content has been converted into sugar, hence their superiority in flavour and sweetness.

The first outdoor sowing in the north is made towards the end of March but, should the weather remain cold, it is better to delay the sowing for ten days; main crop and later maturing varieties should then be sown at fortnightly intervals until the end of May. Early in June, sow a quick maturing early pea to mature early in autumn.

These will provide a succession:

VARIETY	HEIGHT	SOWING TIME	MATURING
Histon Mini	15 inches	November	end May
Early Onward	2 feet	mid-March	mid-June
Kelvedon Monarch	3 feet	end March	end June
Onward	2 feet	early April	mid-July
Histon Maincrop	3 feet	late April	early August
Kelvedon Wonder*	2 feet	May–June	September

* This variety may also be sown in March to mature early

Sowing   The pea enjoys a soil which has been well manured for a previous crop but to grow well, it requires a soil provided with liberal quantities of lime. The finest fertilizer for peas is sewage manure which has been collected over lime, a process which is being gradually discontinued by local authorities. If this is unobtainable, give the ground a liberal dressing of hydrated lime during winter.

It is a moisture retentive soil rather than one rich in nitrogen that the pea requires. An excess of nitrogen will result in an abundance of foliage and large pods containing few peas. To provide humus, used hops are valuable, also anything from the compost heap whilst at planting time, to ensure well filled pods, rake in a 2 oz. per sq. yd. dressing of sulphate of potash and 1 oz. of superphosphate. A light loam, with plenty of humus suits the pea best and a well drained soil is essential for autumn planting. A deeply worked soil is also essential for peas are deep-rooting plants.

A November sowing may be made near a row of broad beans with winter lettuce between. To sow, take out a shallow trench 1–2 in. deep and to the width of a spade. The seeds are planted

A well-staked row of peas. Pea sticks are becoming increasingly hard to obtain, and plastic netting may be used instead

separately, spacing them 2 in. apart to allow the plants room to develop. In this way, a half-pint of seed (peas are sold by the pint) will sow a 10 yd. row. Before filling in the shallow trench, sprinkle peat over the seed and put the covering soil through a sieve to remove any stones which might interfere with plant growth.

With winter sown seed, it is advisable to protect the peas from mice by shaking up the seed-peas in a tin containing red lead and paraffin. Wash the hands and destroy the tin after planting to prevent it from coming into contact with children or animals. To protect the peas from pigeons cover the rows with wire netting pea guards.

To assist germination keep the soil moist and when the plants appear above ground, place twigs on either side of the row to enable the tendrils to take hold early in their growth. Dwarf peas will require only small twiggy sticks but the taller varieties need supporting by tall stakes pressed well into the ground: these should be as high as the plants will grow.

General cultivation   Where pea sticks are difficult to obtain, the rows may be surrounded with netting, held in place by canes or stakes. The plants will pull themselves up the netting and will be prevented from falling on to nearby plants as so often happens when sticks are used. Long lasting green netting made from polypropylene fibre film is satisfactory. After use, the pea haulm should be pulled away and the netting folded and stored in a dry, airy room.

If the soil tends to be heavy, or where gardening in the more exposed parts, peas may be sown in a greenhouse or frame in February and the plants set out early in spring when the soil is friable. So that there is a minimum of root disturbance, sow the peas separately in mini-size decomposable pots, made from sphagnum peat and wood fibre. These are placed in seed trays and the pots filled with John Innes compost after sowing. The plants are set out in their pots 3 in. apart into prepared ground.

The peas will be ready to harvest when the pods are well filled and firm when pressed, but they should not be left until they become hard for they will then have lost both flavour and sweetness. The pods are removed by cutting them from the haulms so as not to pull the plants from the ground. Those lower down the plants are removed first and will allow those at the top to mature later.

PESTS AND DISEASES

FUSARIUM WILT   The most troublesome of pea diseases, the fungus attacking the roots causing the plants to turn yellow and die back. Good cultivation and quick germination of the seed will usually ward off an attack but on land where an outbreak has been known, a resistant variety such as 'Recette' should be grown.

LEAF SPOT   A seed fungus which attacks the leaves, stems and pods causing them to be covered with small brown spots. The pods may fall off before reaching maturity. The disease may be more troublesome in a soil deficient in potash whilst an attack may be prevented from spreading by spraying the foliage with weak Bordeaux Mixture as soon as noticed.

PEA APHIS This attacks most of the legumes and is a 'green fly' which devours the leaf tissues causing both leaves and pods to turn yellow. Dusting with Lindex will prevent an attack or dust with Gamma-BHC before the pods begin to form.

PEA MOTH These moths are troublesome during June and July when they lay their eggs on the flowers. The white larvae eat their way into the pods, devouring the peas. They are eradicated by treating the soil with Aldrin dust before planting and by spraying the plants with Sybol at fortnightly intervals from flowering time and until the first pods have formed.

PRE-EMERGENCE DAMPING OFF In a cold year, the seed may occupy the ground several weeks before germinating and may entirely decay before germination takes place. Treating the peas with Orthocide (including 65 per cent Captan) before sowing will prevent the trouble.

THRIP This pest hibernates in the soil and on pea sticks so the sticks should not be used for a second year. The small steely-black insects feed on the leaves, causing mottling and eventually the leaves turn brown. Dusting the plants with Lindex will give control.

VARIETIES

'EARLY ONWARD' A shorter version of the celebrated 'Onward', bearing blunt-nosed well filled pods of superb flavour.

'HISTON MAINCROP' This grows 2–3 ft. tall and bears, in pairs, large deep green pods well filled with peas of delicious flavour.

'HISTON MINI' Raised by Unwins of Histon, this is a round-seeded variety growing 12–15 in. tall and is suitable for growing under barn cloches. It is a dwarf counterpart of 'Forward', bearing heavily with well filled pods of outstanding flavour.

'KELVEDON MONARCH' It follows 'Early Onward' and grows 2–3 ft. tall, its blunt-ended pods appearing in pairs and filled with 8 or 9 deep green peas which are excellent for freezing.

'KELVEDON WONDER' This grows 18 in. tall and is quick to mature, the dark green pointed pods being well filled with sweet, mild flavoured peas.

'ONWARD' One of the most popular peas ever introduced, a mid-season variety growing 2 ft. tall and bearing, in pairs, dark green blunt-nosed pods filled with 8 or 9 large peas of excellent flavour.

'RECETTE' The introduction of this variety marks a notable advance in pea breeding for its large pointed pods are borne in threes (it being the first triple-podded pea) which makes for larger crops and easier gathering. Resistant to Fusarium Wilt, the pods are ready within 12 weeks of sowing and are filled with 8 or 9 rich green peas of excellent flavour.

Some people resent the time it takes to pod peas, but when you consider that if you buy peas from a shop you pay for the weight of the pods as well, the economics of growing your own make sense

Potato *Solanum tuberosum*

A native of South America, the potato is the staple diet of many countries but nowhere does it grow better than in the cool, moist climate of Britain where more than ten million tons are produced each year.

Apart from its food value, the potato possesses another important quality. That is its ability to crop well in 'dirty' land provided it is well manured. This is land which has become infested with perennial weeds which are often difficult to eradicate. Due to the process of lifting and general cultivations, the soil is cleaned, and after manuring it will be in perfect condition for the planting of other vegetables next year. Again, land of a peaty nature will, if well manured, grow good potatoes which prefer an acid soil. For this reason, soil well limed or of a calcareous nature will produce a crop liable to scab.

A heavy soil, which in a summer of high rainfall will remain wet and cold, may cause the tubers to decay from fungoid diseases so that a clay soil should be brought into condition with quantities of garden compost or decayed strawy manure.

The ground should be made ready during the early winter months, leaving the top soil in a rough condition, to be pulverised by frost and wind.

Starting the tubers The yield of a crop will be increased if the tubers are sprouted before planting, whilst this will ensure the earliest possible crop depending upon soil and situation. With early potatoes, a crop at least 3 weeks earlier than with unsprouted tubers may be expected, whilst with the maincrop a 20 per cent heavier crop may be obtained, due to the longer growing period. The tubers should be clean and even in size.

A frost-proof room is essential for the sprouting but first obtain the tubers or 'seed potatoes' from a reliable grower. They should be 'certified' as having been grown in Scotland or Ireland or on one of the islands situated in the more remote parts of northern Britain. Potatoes grown for seed on high ground in the north of England will be almost as good, being clean and possessing exceptional cropping vigour.

Place the tubers, 'rose' end upwards, close together but not quite touching, in peat 1 in. deep in a shallow wooden box. The tubers should not be cut. The 'rose' end is usually the wide end containing the greatest number of eyes. Place the boxes in a light airy room but not in sunlight whilst frost must be excluded.

When to begin the sprouting will depend upon planting time. In parts of south-west England and Scotland, the early crop is planted in March; elsewhere, mid-April is a suitable time and as the earlies are more tender, it is usual to plant 'late' potatoes (the maincrop) early, and 'early' potatoes late. Sprouting should commence about 6 weeks prior to planting but this will depend upon where the sprouting is to take place and the amount of warmth given. Short sturdy sprouts are required, not more than 1 in. long, otherwise they will break off when planted. Where there are more than two sprouts, the two strongest are retained and all others rubbed out. Do not plant too early; wait until the soil is in a friable condition.

For a heavy crop, take out a trench to a depth of 9 in. and make the trenches 2 ft. apart to allow for 'earthing'. At the bottom place 3 in. of decayed manure or material from the compost heap and over this, 3 in. of peat. Into the peat, the tubers are carefully pressed 2 ft. apart, the sprouts (or eyes if not sprouted) uppermost and about 4 in. below the top of the trench. Before covering them with soil, place more peat around the tubers or use soil which has been passed through a fine riddle.

To the soil to be used to fill up the trench, give a 2 oz. per sq. yd. dressing of superphosphate of lime and sulphate of potash mixed together. This will increase the yield, encourage earlier maturity and help the plants to resist disease. The mixture should be in the proportion of 2 parts superphosphate to 1 part potash. Nitrogenous fertilizers should not be used for they tend to make for excessive top growth and a 'soft' tuber.

On low-lying land of a heavy nature, the tubers should be planted on ridges, in V-fashion. At the top of the ridge, a drill 6 in. deep is made and lined with peat. Into this the tubers are pressed and the drill filled in with finely riddled soil containing the superphosphate and potash. Never plant potatoes too close together or the haulm (the leaves and stems) will grow weak which will mean a reduced crop.

It is important to plant potatoes in an open, sunny position so that the plants may obtain the maximum of sunshine. Make the rows from north to south, to allow both sides of the rows to receive the same amount of sunlight. If possible, early potatoes should be given a southerly slope and as light a soil as possible.

For an early crop in the more exposed gardens, an early variety may be planted in a frame over a mild hot bed. A 6-in. depth of compost is placed in the frame and on top is placed a 6-in. depth of riddled soil into which the tubers are planted with a trowel, spacing them 9 in. apart and just covering them with soil. Water in and cover with lights. Should there be frost about, cover the lights with sacking at night and remove by day. If the tubers are planted about mid-March, they will yield a useful crop of 'new' potatoes at the end of May. If the haulm is earthed up with a peat and soil mixture this will help to prevent loss of moisture about the tubers as the days become warmer.

As the foliage appears above the soil, it should be earthed up about 3 in. and again a month later to a similar depth. This will prevent the foliage from being damaged during cultivations. At the same time and as a precaution against 'Blight', spray the foliage with Bordeaux Mixture.

Harvesting Lift when the foliage begins to die down, though where the crop is required to eat at home, lifting of the early varieties may commence in June, and the maincrop towards the end of August. If earlies, second earlies and maincrop varieties have been planted, there will be tubers to harvest from June until October when the winter supply will be available from storage.

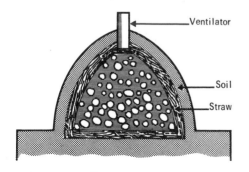

Diagram of a well-made potato clamp. Ventilation is essential to the success of the clamp

Ventilator

Soil

Straw

Lift the tubers with a fork, taking care to place it well away from the plant for the tubers spread out and are easily damaged by careless lifting. Potatoes lifted early should be kept under the stairs or in a cellar away from light, otherwise they will turn green.

'New' potatoes may be enjoyed all the year round if a quantity are placed in a metal biscuit tin filled with dry peat and buried 12 in. deep in the garden, a stone marking the position.

After lifting, burn the haulm so as not to perpetuate disease which would contaminate the garden compost heap.

PESTS AND DISEASES

BLACK LEG   Bacterial rot of potato tubers may be troublesome in a wet season. The disease starts at the end of a tuber causing slimy areas and, when cut, emits an unpleasant smell. Clean seed will do much to prevent an outbreak whilst it is preferable to plant whole tubers rather than cut portions.

BLIGHT   Dangerous if it takes hold but is easily prevented by spraying the foliage in early July and again a month later with Bordeaux Mixture. Blight attacks the leaves as brown spots; later the whole plant turns brown whilst the tubers are also damaged, sunken areas appearing.

COLORADO BEETLE   Rare in Britain, it is so destructive to potatoes that it is a 'notifiable' pest, i.e. its occurrence must be reported to the Ministry of Agriculture. It has orange and black striped wings and when fully grown measures $\frac{1}{2}$ in. long. It winters in the soil and lays its orange eggs on the plants. The grubs are also orange and where in numbers will quickly wipe out a plantation. As a precaution, treat the soil with Aldrin dust before planting.

EELWORM   This pest attacks the tubers causing them to become a slimy mass whilst the foliage turns yellow and dies back. There is no known cure and badly infested land should be rested from potatoes for four years. Where they have caused only limited trouble, treat the soil with Jeyes Fluid at a strength of 2 tablespoons to 1 gal. of water a month before planting.

LEAF SCORCH   Due to potash deficiency, the leaves curling at the margins. Later, bronze and yellow blotches appear. A light application of sulphate of potash at planting time will prevent an outbreak.

SCAB   This attacks the tubers in the form of rough, scab-like spots and, where the infestation is severe, the scabs may cover the whole surface. It is prevalent only on land of a calcareous nature. Green manuring before planting potatoes, by sowing and digging in rape when 2 in. high will do much to prevent an outbreak.

WART DISEASE   A 'notifiable' disease and on infected land only wart-immune varieties such as 'Arran Pilot' (early) and 'Dr McIntosh' (maincrop) should be grown. It first attacks the stems and lower leaves but it is usually found only on the tubers which upon lifting may have the appearance of cauliflower-like structures.

VARIETIES

First Early

'ARRAN PILOT'   One of the earliest to mature, it crops heavily, its white kidney-shaped tubers having outstanding flavour.

'EPICURE'   Very early, it stands cold weather better than any early potato and is a round white of delicious flavour.

'HOME GUARD'   A round white with shallow eyes and cropping heavily, the tubers growing uniform in size making it ideal for exhibition.

Second Early

'CRAIG'S ROYAL'   A kidney potato with a soft pale creamy-pink skin with darker pink around the shallow eyes. It bears a heavy crop and is good for exhibition.

A well-grown crop of potatoes. To lift the crop without damaging the tubers the fork should be inserted beside the row, not in the middle of it

'DUNBAR ROVER' Immune to Wart Disease, this is a reliable cropper for a light soil, the oval-shaped tubers being pure white, delicious when baked in their skins.

'SUTTON'S OLYMPIC' Though early to mature, this will keep through winter, whilst it crops heavily in all parts of Britain, the tubers being round and pink skinned.

Maincrop

'DR MCINTOSH' Producing a larger number of uniform tubers per plant than any other variety, this requires a long season to mature. The long white kidney-shaped tubers have shallow eyes and are borne in abundance.

'PENTLAND CROWN' Raised in Scotland, it is a round variety with a cream skin and handsome rust markings. It crops heavily in all soils.

Radish *Raphanus sativus*

Radishes require growing quickly otherwise they will be hard and woody and, to have them sweet and succulent, the turnip-rooted varieties should be no larger than a 1p piece; those of tapering form no longer than the thickness of one's little finger. Used in this manner, they will be juicy and nut-like. If grown slowly or left too long in the seed bed, radishes will be bitter and stringy.

General cultivation The seed bed should contain some humus to retain summer moisture and old mushroom bed compost is ideal, or work into the soil a mixture of peat and decayed farmyard manure. Early in March, bring the bed to a fine tilth and when the soil is friable, sow thinly and preferably broadcast, raking the seed into the top inch of soil.

During dry weather, keep the ground moist and the radishes will be ready to use within a month of sowing. To maintain a succession, make a sowing once a month until early September and, for winter use, sow in July the 'China Rose' and 'Winter Black' radishes.

Winter radishes are sown in drills 9 in. apart, the Black being thinned to 6 in. in the rows for they grow as large as a turnip. Keep the soil moist during summer and give an occasional watering with liquid manure. The roots are lifted early in November and are stored in sand until required.

PESTS AND DISEASES

CLUB ROOT   The swelling of the tap root may be due to this common disease of brassicas and may be prevented by treating the seed, or the soil, with calomel dust before sowing.

RADISH FLY   The pest lays its eggs in the soil, the larvae attacking the roots. Dusting the ground with Lindex before sowing will prevent an attack but Lindex must not come into contact with potatoes.

TURNIP FLY   This is a troublesome foe but may be kept away by dusting the ground and the plants with derris, shortly after the seed has germinated.

VARIETIES

'FRENCH BREAKFAST'   An intermediate variety, the elongated roots being bright red tipped with white. The market growers' favourite as it makes a striking bunch.

'ICICLE'   The long tapering root of this variety is like a white transparent icicle and remains crisp, cold and juicy longer than any other variety.

'INCA'   A new radish which forms a cherry-like globe and which reveals a crisp white flesh when of large size. Sliced, it makes for delicious eating.

'CHINA ROSE' In appearance, this is tubular, like a large 'French Breakfast', thickening towards the base. The colour is bright rosy-red with the flesh white and crisp. It is delicious sliced and used with Lamb's Lettuce and cream cheese in a brown bread sandwich.

'WINTER BLACK' It forms a large round root covered in a jet black skin. The flesh is white and succulent and has a distinct nutty taste. It may be sliced or grated for use in a winter salad.

Savoy *Brassica oleracea bullata sabauda*

The largest heading cabbages and the hardiest of all, being at their best in the New Year after being subjected to frost, which makes them crisp and tender. Their crinkled and deeply veined leaves enable winter rains to drain away quickly so that the hearts never become wet and soggy. Their curled leaves are similar to those of kale when cooked.

Savoys require a long growing season and a well manured soil. Sow early in April, in shallow drills and plant out in May 2 ft. apart. The plants will occupy the ground until the following spring and require a soil containing plenty of humus and nitrogenous manure. Strawy manure or shoddy suits this plant well and the ground should have been well limed in winter. If not, rake in 4 oz. per sq. yd. of nitro-chalk before planting.

VARIETIES

'OMEGA' The latest to mature, forming a large blue-green head which stands well and is extremely hardy. May be cut as late as April.

'SAVOY KING' A hybrid bearing large flat heads, uniform in size and weighing 4 lb. each. The heads begin to heart at an early age so that they may be used over a long period. It also resists heat better than any other savoy and will crinkle well.

Savoy cabbages are not grown as often as they should be. They have beautiful glaucous foliage, and could well be grown for their foliage in the flower border

'TOM THUMB' The best for a small garden for it makes a miniature head which is sweet and succulent and of darkest green. As it matures quickly, two sowings should be made, one in April to heart before Christmas, another a month later to mature in the New Year.

Shallot *Allium ascalonicum*

Grown chiefly for pickling, shallots require a light soil containing humus, preferably in the form of decayed manure or old mushroom bed compost. Bring the soil to a fine tilth and, before planting which should be early in March, rake in 2 oz. per sq. yd. of sulphate of potash and roll or tread to ensure a firm bed.

Plant when the soil is in a suitable condition, merely pressing the sets (as the small bulbs are called) into the surface, in no way covering them. Set them 10 in. apart and keep the soil moist. Feeding with dilute liquid manure will help to build up a large crop and enhance the quality of the bulbs.

Harvesting Towards the end of August, bend over the necks to encourage the bulbs to ripen, when towards the end of September, the clusters of small bulbs are lifted and dried. They should be pickled within a month of drying if their full flavour is to be preserved.

It is always preferable to plant sets rather than to raise seedlings which are often wiped out by onion fly whilst seedlings rarely have time to reach full maturity in an ordinary British summer.

The finest variety is 'Dutch Yellow', the offsets being harvested in Holland where they have a longer ripening season and are stored under ideal conditions.

Spinach *Spinacea oleracea*

This plant is not a universal favourite, nor is it very successful in the garden, for summer spinach readily runs to seed, whilst plants of winter spinach may decay in excessively damp weather, but the plant has health giving qualities and many appreciate its unique 'earthy' flavour.

Summer spinach is best grown from a succession of sowings made from the end of March and every three weeks until late in July. To prevent the plants running to seed, select a position of partial shade and provide a humus laden soil. The plants require a rich diet and should be grown as cool as possible.

As the plants are required to produce an abundance of leaf, dig into the soil some nitrogenous manure, augmented by a $\frac{1}{2}$ oz. per sq. yd. dressing of nitrate of soda to be given as soon as the plants begin to grow.

Sowing Sow the seed in shallow drills made 12 in. apart and thin the plants to 9 in. in the rows. It is the round leaf varieties that are sown for summer use, the leaves being gathered when young and tender. As soon as the plants run to seed, grub them up. Copious amounts of moisture in summer will delay the plants from seeding and an occasional watering with dilute liquid manure will improve the quality and extend the season.

Hoeing between the rows will keep the soil aerated and suppress weeds. It should be said that winter spinach should not be too heavily cut or the plants may be harmed by frost.

PESTS AND DISEASES

DOWNY MILDEW   This disease is recognized by the pale yellow spots on the upper surface of the leaves and the blue-grey mildew which forms on the underside. The fungus may winter in the soil so rotational cropping is desirable. Dust the plants with flowers of sulphur if an outbreak is noticed but the best way to prevent an attack is to soak spinach seed in 1 per cent copper sulphate solution for 2 hours and then to dry off before sowing.

VARIETIES

Summer

'CLEANLEAF'   Of recent introduction, its smooth dark green leaves are rounded at the ends and held well above the soil on a long stalk so that washing is not necessary.

'MONSTROUS VIROFLAY'   Strangely named yet it is one of the best for summer use, making a large plant with an abundance of smooth round leaves.

'SUPERB'   A new variety of good leaf quality and highly resistant to downy mildew, the most troublesome of spinach diseases. The medium green leaves are held well above the soil.

Winter

'BLOOMSDALE LONG-STANDING'   Hardy long-standing for winter use, the dark green leaves being large, extensively crinkled and held well above the soil, remaining in rosette form for several weeks.

'NEW ZEALAND' (*Tetragonia-expansa*)   Botanically unrelated to the spinach, this is quite distinct in its habit, forming a low spreading plant and producing an abundance of thick fleshy leaves. It is untroubled by warm, dry weather whilst the leaves and young stem tips may be picked throughout summer and autumn and well into winter.

Spinach 'Victoria Longstanding Summer'. A very fine-flavoured summer spinach with a large edible leaf, and slow to run to seed. 'Victoria Longstanding Winter' is a winter equivalent. *Courtesy Thompson & Morgan (Ipswich) Limited*

Swede   *Brassica napus* var. *naprobrassica*

In the United States it is called Rutabaga and is considered to have a better flavour than the turnip from which it is distinguished by the deep yellow flesh. Swedes are hardier than turnips and may be left in the ground during winter to be lifted when required. They are delicious boiled and mashed with butter and served with meats.

Sowing   Seed is sown early in May, in drills made 18 in. apart, the seedlings thinned to 9 in. in the rows for they grow larger than turnips. Thinning should be done as soon as the seedlings are large enough to handle. Water copiously during dry weather for this is a plant that will make growth and remain free from stringiness only if supplies of moisture are available.

The roots may be used when of tennis ball size when they are especially sweet and succulent. They will reach maturity

114

by mid-October and may be lifted and stored in a cellar or shed and covered with straw, or they may be lifted whenever required. The flavour will be improved after being subjected to hard frost.

They suffer from the same pests and diseases as turnips.

VARIETY

'PURPLE-TOP YELLOW' The finest variety, the globe-shaped roots are coloured purple at the top whilst the sweet, closely grained flesh cooks to deepest orange.

Tomato *Lycopersicon esculentum*

Tomatoes, or Love Apples, as they were once called, were introduced into Europe shortly after the journeys of Columbus to the New World.

To grow them outdoors, a warm friable soil is essential and the ground should be trenched. Soil to a depth of about 15 in. is removed and into the trench should be placed plenty of plant food. Farmyard manure is not as easily available as it used to be but if some can be acquired it should be incorporated into the trench or added to compost which is to be dug into the trench. This is obtained by composting a quantity of straw with an activator, to which is added some dry poultry manure to assist in fermentation. If the heap is stacked as high as possible to allow it to heat up quickly and turned at weekly intervals for three weeks, a very useful compost for tomatoes will result.

Soil preparation It is an excellent plan to place in the trenches a straw compost that is only half composted, for fairly long straw will help greatly with the aeration of the trench soil, a free circulation of air being necessary for a healthy rooting system. Or stand straw on end in the trench and sprinkle sulphate of ammonia over it. It will then begin its decomposition before the top soil is added.

Horticultural peat and hop manure mixed together will also contribute to the humus content of the soil and should be used where possible. Chopped seaweed is also an excellent organic fertilizer. Shoddy (cloth waste) is also valuable, especially when used in conjunction with partially composted straw. In all but the very lightest soils peat should be used in quantity, and again for mulching the plants when the fruits begin to form. Should it not be possible to compost a quantity of straw, then it would be advisable to place lawn mowings and garden refuse at the bottom of the trench.

When the humus content of the trenches is established, and this will decompose either in a compost heap or in the trenches themselves during winter, the base fertilizers are added. The humus forming materials should have been covered over with 2 in. of soil and trodden down. This treading will prevent air pockets forming but, where straw is present, treading will not cut off air circulation. Early in spring, the base fertilizers may then be mixed with the top soil before it is placed in the trenches.

Another important requirement of the tomato is potash. Poultry manure which has been stored dry before using in the compost heap contains almost ten times the potash of farmyard manure, and where guano or poultry droppings have been used in this way, almost no extra potash will be needed. Where farmyard manure only is being used and then only on a small scale, it will be necessary to give potash additions.

To counteract any tendency of the plants to suffer from lack of magnesium, which in recent years has become prevalent, a sprinkling of Epsom Salts (magnesium sulphate) should be forked in at planting time.

Raising the plants It is realized that not everyone possesses a heated greenhouse and will either have to purchase plants, well hardened off, for planting out early in May under cloches, or early in June when growing in the open.

The seed is individually sown spacing it 2 in. apart and just covering it with soil. It is watered and the light placed over the frame. Water sparingly, and as soon as germination has taken place the seedlings should be given ventilation on all suitable occasions.

When they have formed their first pair of leaves they should be moved to 3-in. pots containing the John Innes potting compost and grown on for 3–4 weeks before hardening and planting outside.

The plants should be set out 3–4 ft. apart early in June and in a position of full sun where there is some protection from prevailing winds. Plant firmly and water well, henceforth keeping the soil comfortably moist. Bud-drop will result if the soil is too dry. Plants which are growing on in large pots where they are to crop will require careful attention as to watering, for the soil will dry out more quickly.

Plants in the open ground must also be watered with care, otherwise the soil will be thrown up on to the foliage or flower trusses, with the possible result that such troublesome diseases as Botrytis and Buckeye Rot may be the outcome. The bush tomatoes are more liable to suffer in this respect owing to their dwarf habit, and many growers place a layer of clean straw under each plant about 3 weeks after they have been set out. This not only prevents splashing of the foliage and trusses but prevents the soil drying out.

Pollinating Pollinating the trusses by carefully brushing each flower with a small camel-hair brush, or even with a few hen's feathers tied lightly together at the end of a small stick will assist in the formation of fruit. This procedure should take place around mid-day, when the flowers are open and when all moisture is off the flowers, so it is advisable to withhold over-head syringeing until after hand pollinating has been done.

Outdoor plants cannot be pollinated when they are wet from rain or mist and an appropriate time must be awaited.

Bringing on the crop Those varieties of dwarf habit such as 'Atom' and 'Tiny Tim' will require neither 'stopping' nor the removal of side shoots. They 'stop' themselves.

Those of taller habit should be 'stopped' at the fourth truss so that they will be able to ripen their fruit before the autumn.

As an aid to ripening, a light dressing of sulphate of potash, 2 oz. per sq. yd. could be given just before mulching and, from the end of July until mid-September, a weekly application of dilute manure water will maintain the nourishment required by the later maturing fruit.

Defoliation also calls for attention. No leaves should be removed until they have completed their part in the health of the plant, for the function of foliage is just as important as root action.

PESTS AND DISEASES

BLIGHT   This is the same fungus that attacks the potato causing a grey mould to cover the underside of the leaves. With tomatoes it causes dark brown spots on the leaves and grey patches on the green fruits. It is rare on plants in heated houses, troubling mostly those growing without heat or outdoors in a wet, sunless summer. Spraying the plants with Burgundy Mixture once every 3 weeks from the time for the first fruit sets will prevent an outbreak.

BOTRYTIS   This fungus disease is caused by careless watering splashing the soil on to the lower leaves: it will spread rapidly under cold, damp conditions or those of excessive humidity. Too close planting should be avoided. The disease is diagnosed by the appearance of brown tissue which will spread to the calyces, causing the fruit to fall prematurely. Spraying with Shirlan AG at the first sign will usually give control.

CLADOSPORUM   Also known as Leaf Mould or Leaf Spot, the disease appears as small yellow spots on the underside of the leaves. As it spreads, the whole leaf becomes a mass of brown mould whilst the fruits fall away without maturing. Spraying with a copper-oil compound will prevent it from destroying the plant tissues if caught in time but this should not be done until early July, until the plant is well established. It is advisable to plant resistant varieties.

WHITE FLY   Like a tiny white moth this is a dreaded pest amongst indoor tomatoes though it may be controlled by introducing to the greenhouse the white fly parasite supplied by several agricultural stations. Wettable DDT sprayed on to the plants once every 3 weeks from the time the first fruit has set will give control.

VARIETIES *(Red)*

'ATOM'   Of almost prostrate habit and making little foliage, the plant needs neither staking nor stopping. When once the

Tomatoes are probably the most rewarding of all vegetables to grow.
A good crop is a joy to look at and a joy to eat – something any grower can
be rightly proud of

fruit has formed, it ripens very fast with the minimum amount
of sunshine. Owing to its low habit it is the best of all tomatoes
for an exposed garden, and may be brought into fruit by
early July if planted under barn-type cloches or in frames.

Atom is not a large fruit, about the size of a golf ball.
It ripens without any trace of 'greenback' and, apart from
feeding with liquid manure each week, it requires no other
attention.

'GOLDEN JUBILEE'   Bearing a large fruit of brightest yellow
with the flesh almost the colour of an orange, this is a new
and splendid variety. The habit of the plant is stiff and short
jointed.

'HISTON CROPPER'   Of dwarf habit and making little foliage,
it carries a heavy crop of medium sized fruit with a unique
'tart' flavour. The crop ripens quickly in the minimum of
sunshine. The plant is highly resistant to blight.

'HISTON EARLY' Raised by Unwins of Histon, this is the earliest and heaviest cropping of the taller growing outdoor varieties. The plant is short-jointed with large potato-like leaves, the fruit being bright red, even in size and of excellent flavour.

Growing indoors The introduction of a number of varieties of hybrid vigour which, combined with a resistance to many of the destructive tomato diseases of the past, has revolutionized indoor tomato culture during recent years.

Light intensity will play an important part in planting for an early crop. Those living near to the south coast, where there is a higher rate of winter sunshine than elsewhere in Britain, may plant in a heated house towards the end of February, seed having been sown about mid-December. In the Home Counties, planting may be done early in March and on the east coast of Yorkshire where there are large commercial plantings, mid-March is the accepted time. It is incorrect to think that growers in the less favourable districts can obtain equally early crops merely by increasing the house temperature, for this would result only in 'drawn' plants. To grow early tomatoes, there must also be sufficient warmth to keep the plants growing whatever the weather. This will mean a minimum temperature of 50 °F during day time and 45 °F at night. Until these temperatures can be ensured, planting must be delayed.

In a cool house, planting should not be done before the first week of April in the south; mid-April in the Midlands; and the month end in the north. Again, the plants must be kept growing without check but if warmth can be provided at night by a paraffin oil heater or by electric heating, then planting may be done a fortnight earlier.

Tomatoes may be grown on the greenhouse bench, planting either in boxes or in wooden troughs made at the back. The plants may be trained up the roof, being supported on long canes fastened to wires stretched across the roof; or in a Dutch-light house they may be planted directly into ground beds of prepared compost or in large earthenware pots placed on the floor. In a Dutch-light house the glass will reach down to the base, so that the plants will receive the maximum amount of light. Tomatoes may also be grown in deep boxes placed in rows on the greenhouse floor. The hybrids should be planted 18–20 in. apart, allowing them more room than ordinary varieties for they make plenty of leaf and form large trusses of fruit.

Sowing Where raising seedlings, the first sowings are made early in January and, where electricity is available, a simple propagating frame will be a necessity to maintain a temperature of 65 °F in the south (where there is a greater intensity of light). Germination will take 7–8 days. In less favourable areas, the temperature should not exceed 60 °F, when germination will take 10–12 days.

Seed is sown in boxes or pans containing John Innes compost and the propagating unit will provide the correct humidity. Sow thinly, spacing out the seed so that the seedlings will not be crowded. When they have formed their first two pairs of leaves, transplant to small pots or to Root-o-Pots made of compressed peat and filled with the John Innes potting compost. There will be no further root disturbance for the plants may be set out in their fruiting quarters in the 'pots'.

The seedlings and young plants should be kept growing on in a temperature of 58 °F, falling to 50 °F at night. The atmosphere should be moist but buoyant; tomatoes will not tolerate 'stuffy' conditions. The plants must be kept moist and, for their watering, always use water heated to the temperature of the greenhouse. Water used from the tap will cause chilling which will bring about a check in plant growth. Well grown seedlings will set heavy first trusses and early tomatoes are always most in demand. Should the plants take on a 'blue' appearance, this may be due to cold conditions and may be corrected by increasing the temperature by several degrees; alternatively it may be due to lack of phosphates in the soil. This can be overcome by watering with $\frac{1}{2}$ oz. of superphosphate of lime dissolved in a gallon of water. Do not keep the plants in the pots too long before moving to their fruiting quarters or they may show signs of lacking in nutriment.

If planting in ground beds, double digging to a depth of 2 ft. should be done, incorporating peat, decayed manure and garden compost. Tomatoes love peat for they like a soil with a pH value of about 6 which is slightly acid. A too alkaline soil will produce a light crop. To guard against wireworm, dust the soil with Lindex as it is prepared.

Where growing in pots, a compost should be made up containing fibrous turf loam, preferably of a heavy nature but containing plenty of root fibres. Into this some decayed manure should be mixed, together with some peat or bark fibre to aerate the compost. To each barrowful of compost, mix in 1 lb. of steamed bone flour and some sulphate of potash, at the rate of $\frac{1}{2}$ oz. for each pot. A 10 in. pot should be used and before filling with compost, it must be well crocked. Allow 2 in. from the top of the compost to the pot rim so that a mulch can be given when the first four trusses have formed. Plant firmly and water in. Maintain a buoyant atmosphere by ventilating on all suitable days and, when the weather is warm, syringe the foliage frequently and water the floor of the greenhouse. Up to mid-May, the ventilators should be closed at night but from then onwards may be left open day and night except when cold.

The lower (first) trusses will be opening their flowers when there are few insects about and should be assisted in their pollination by dusting them with a camel-hair brush. This is done about mid-day and the fertilization will be more successful if a misty atmosphere is created in the house afterwards. Spraying the plants should continue throughout summer, not only to assist with pollination but to prevent excessive moisture evaporation from the foliage.

Water the soil only when necessary until the first truss has formed; then, as the fruits appear and begin to swell, give ever increasing supplies, keeping the soil always damp. If the soil is allowed to dry out, and this is followed by heavy watering, it will cause the fruits to burst their skin.

When 12 in. tall, the plants should be supported by 8 ft. canes to which they are loosely tied with raffia and, from this time onwards, all side growths which appear from the leaf axils should be removed by pinching out. Or use a sharp knife, taking care not to damage the main stems.

The plants will be ready for a mulch in June, a month later where growing in a cold greenhouse. A mixture of turf loam, peat and decayed manure will prove suitable. It should be given to a depth of about 2 in. around the base of the plants and the surface roots will at once begin to grow into it with the

Tomatoes being grown in the greenhouse by the straw-bale method of culture. The advantage of this method is that it minimizes the risk of tomato soil-sickness

plant growing away with renewed vigour. These new roots will take up additional moisture and nutriment needed by the plant in forming its top trusses. A $\frac{1}{2}$ oz. per sq. yd. dressing of sulphate of potash given each plant in July will help the fruit to ripen well and prevent 'greenback'; or give a dressing of five parts nitro-chalk and one part potash which will keep the plants growing on and will help the fruit to ripen. Feeding once a week with dilute liquid manure will help to maintain the vigour of the plants and increase the yield. Shortage of magnesium will also reduce the weight of crop. This may be corrected by watering once every 3 weeks with magnesium sulphate (1 oz. to a gallon of water). As the fruit swells, the trusses should be supported by loosely tying them to the cane with raffia.

The correct time to stop the plants also calls for judgement, depending upon variety and the season. In a cold, dull summer it may be necessary to stop after six or seven trusses for the top fruit to ripen, whereas in a year of prolonged sunshine plants of the hybrids may be grown on to twelve or fourteen trusses before stopping. If the plants are stopped too soon they will not bear their maximum crop; if stopped too late, they will not bring their top trusses to maturity.

After stopping, the defoliation of the plant can begin. First, the lower leaves are removed and, as a rule, only the foliage below a truss is cut away when the fruit has matured. Then as the next truss ripens, the foliage below that truss can be removed and so on. Thus, the whole plant is defoliated to coincide with the ripening of the last truss. Too early removal of the foliage must be guarded against as this will upset the balance of the plant.

VARIETIES

'AMBERLEY CROSS' Raised at the Glasshouse Research Institute at Littlehampton and resistant to 'greenback', it is the earliest to ripen in a warm greenhouse and crops heavily. It makes a tall, leafy plant and though setting heavy first trusses, it continues to grow with vigour and bears high class fruit until the end of autumn.

'EUROCROSS' A hybrid of the 'Moneymaker' type producing non-greenback fruits of excellent quality. Immune to Cladosporum and a heavy cropper, its fruits are of excellent quality, shape and size.

124

'INFINITY CROSS' The introduction of this cultivar heralds something of major importance in hybrid tomatoes for it has yielded up to 20 lb. of fruit per plant in an amateur's greenhouse and a single truss of 8 lb. has been recorded. As the trusses are so large, only six should be allowed from plants grown in a warm house and only four from cold house plants. It is necessary to feed heavily. The fruits are round and of medium size and ripen without trace of greenback.

'KELVEDON CROSS' This does well in a cold or a heated house, its trusses being closely spaced, the even-sized globular fruits ripening evenly and early with no trace of greenback.

Turnip *Brassica rapa*

By planting for succession, it is possible to have turnips throughout the year.

For an early crop, seed of 'Early White Milan' or 'Tokyo Cross' should be sown in a frame over a gentle hot bed at the end of February. Sow thinly and space the seedlings 6 in. apart, removing any which might cause overcrowding. Admit plenty of air when the seed has germinated, and keep the soil moist. By early May, the roots will have attained the size of small tennis balls and will be ready to use.

This is a valuable 'catch' crop for the market grower, for there are few fresh vegetables in the shops in May. They are tied in bunches of eight or nine turnips.

Outdoors, a sowing is made early in April, between dwarf peas, to mature early in July. Here again, the roots are lifted when reaching tennis ball size, before they become coarse and woody.

Turnips require a rich, deeply worked soil which has been well limed and a firm seed bed containing plenty of wood ash. Sow broadcast and thin to 6 in. apart. Like radishes, turnips need to grow quickly so that they must never be allowed to lack moisture.

To mature early outdoors, 'Early Snowball' is recommended and this should be followed by a sowing made early July of 'Utility' or 'Golden Ball' to provide roots for winter use. Sown in July, the roots will have reached about 4 in. across by winter time and this is the size when they are at their best for culinary use. They are completely hardy and may be lifted as required.

If sowing in drills, make them 12 in. apart and space the seedlings to 6 in. apart in the rows. If the turnips are wanted for winter storing, they should be lifted early in December, the leaves being cut off but not the roots.

PESTS AND DISEASES

CLUB ROOT   This attacks all the brassicas, the turnip being no exception. Well limed land will rarely support the disease and dusting the soil with calomel before the seed is sown will give protection.

TURNIP FLY   This is a beetle which attacks the plants in the seedling stage, laying its eggs on the leaves in May. The grubs eat into the leaf tissues whilst the last of the three cycles which are produced each season winter in the soil as pupae. Before sowing, seed should be treated with a combined dressing whilst the young plants should be dusted with derris on a dry, sunny day towards the end of May and again a month later.

VARIETIES

'EARLY MILAN'   A distinct variety with strap-like leaves, this is the first to mature. The roots are flattened and are white with a purple top.

'EARLY SNOWBALL'   A white globe-shaped turnip with sweet and tender flesh and fine for exhibition.

'GOLDEN BALL'   This stands through winter and is the finest for late summer sowing. The roots are ball-shaped and bright orange with the distinctive flavour of a swede.

'TOKYO CROSS'   An F1 hybrid maturing early and showing high resistance to disease. The pure white globe-shaped roots reach a diameter of 3 in. in 5 weeks and will grow to double the size without becoming woody.

Index